The History of Bread From Pre-historic to Modern Times

THE HISTORY OF BREAD

EGYPTIANS THRESHING CORN BY HAND.

EGYPTIANS WINNOWING AND STORING CORN IN SACKS, AND A SCRIBE
NOTING THE QUANTITIES

The History of Bread

From Pre-historic to Modern Times

BY

JOHN ASHTON

LONDON

BROOKE HOUSE PUBLISHING CO.

BROOKE HOUSE

22, 23, 39, WARWICK LANE, and 2, STATIONERS'
HALL COURT, E.C.

LONDON:
PRINTED BY WILLIAM CLOWES AND SONS, LIMITED,
DUKE STREET, STAMFORD STREET, S.E., AND GREAT WINDMILL STREET, W.

PREFACE

IT seems extraordinary, but it is, nevertheless, a fact, that, up to this present time, there has not been written, in the English language, a History of *Bread*, although it is called 'the Staff of Life,' and really is a large staple of food.

There have been small *brochures* on the subject, and large volumes on the Chemistry of Bread, its making and baking; and long controversies as to the merits of whole meal, and other kindred questions, but no History. It is to remedy this that I have written this book, in which I have endeavoured to trace Bread from Pre-historic to Modern Times.

JOHN ASHTON.

CONTENTS

LIST OF ILLUSTRATIONS

THE
HISTORY OF BREAD

FROM PRE-HISTORIC TO MODERN TIMES.

CHAPTER I.

PRE-HISTORIC BREAD.

MAN, as is evidenced by his teeth, was created graminivorous, as well as carnivorous, and the earliest skull yet found possesses teeth exactly the same as modern man, the carnivorous teeth not being bigger, whilst in many cases the whole of the teeth have been worn down, as if by masticating hard substances, such as parched grain.

In the history of bread, the lake dwellings of Switzerland are most useful, as from them we can gather the cereals their inhabitants used, their bread, and the implements with which they crushed the corn. The men who lived in them are the earliest known civilised inhabitants of Europe—by which I mean that they cultivated several kinds of cereals— wove cloth, made mats, baskets, and fishing nets, and, besides, baked bread.

The cereals known to us, and made use of, are the result of much cultivation, improved by selection;

The History of Bread

and Hallett's pedigree wheat would be hardly recognised when put by the side of its humble progenitor of pre-historic times. We now use wheat, barley, oats, Indian corn or maize, rye, rice, millet, and Guinea corn, or Indian millet, besides such odds and ends as the sea lyme grass (*Elymus arenarius*), which, though uncultivated, affords seed which is used in Iceland as a food, for want of something better.

We have been enabled to trace with certainty the cereals used by pre-historic man, as they have been found lying in the lake mud, or buried under a bed of peat several feet thick, when they had to be collected out of a soft, dark-coloured mud, which formed the ancient lake-bottom, and is now called the relic bed. Dr. Oswald Heer, in his *Treatise on the Plants of the Lake Dwellings*, says : 'Stones and pottery, domestic implements and charcoal ashes, grains of corn and bones, lie together in a confused mass. And yet they are by no means spread regularly over the bottom, but are frequently found in patches. The places where bones are plentiful, where the seeds of raspberries and blackberries, and the stones of sloes and cherries are found in heaps, probably indicate where there were holes in the wooden platform, through which the refuse was thrown into the lake ; whilst those places where burnt fruits, bread, and plaited and woven cloth are found, indicate the position of store rooms in the very places where they were burnt, and thus the contents fell into the water. The burnt fruits and seeds, therefore, unquestionably belong to the age of the lake dwellings ; and a portion of them are in very good preservation, for the process of burning has not essentially changed their form. Many of the remains of plants, however, have been preserved in an unburnt state.'

He gives the following list of cereals that have been found, and it is a somewhat extensive one: '(1) Small lake-dwelling barley (*Hordeum hexastichum sanctum*), (2) Compact six-rowed barley (*Hordeum hexastichum densum*), (3) Two-rowed barley (*Hordeum distichum*), (4) Small lake-dwelling wheat (*Triticum vulgare antiquorum*), (5) Beardless compact wheat (*Triticum vulgare compactum muticum*), (6) Egyptian wheat (*Triticum turgidum*), (7) Spelt (*Triticum spelta*), (8) Two-grained wheat (*Triticum dicoccum*), (9) One-grained wheat (*Triticum mono coccum*), (10) Rye (*Secale cereale*), (11) Oat (*Avena sativa*), (12) Millet (*Panicum miliaceum*), and (13) Italian millet (*Setaria Italicum*).'

Of these Nos. 1 and 4 were the most ancient, most important, and most generally cultivated, and next to them come Nos. 5, 12, and 13. Nos. 6, 8, and 9 were, probably, like No. 3, only cultivated, as experiments, in a few places. Nos. 7 and 11 appeared later, not until the Bronze Age, whilst No. 10 (rye) was entirely unknown amongst the lake dwellings of Switzerland.

At the lake settlement at Wangen a remarkable quantity of charred corn was dug up. Mr. Löhle believes that, altogether, and at various times, he has collected as much as 100 bushels. Sometimes he found the entire ears, at other times the grain only. Any of my readers can see for themselves some of this wheat, and also some raspberry seeds, found at Wangen. In the same case in the Pre-historic Saloon of the British Museum may be seen specimens of beans, peas, charred straw, acorns, hazel nuts, barley in the ear, millet in ear, in seed, and made into cakes, one showing the pattern of the bottom of a basket, and another the impress of a rush mat. The cakes or bread of millet are very solid, and are made of meal coarsely crushed.

We know how this was crushed, for we have found their corn-crushers and mealing-stones. Of these the rude corn-crushers are undoubtedly the earliest. These stones, with their rounded ends, for a time somewhat puzzled the archæologist as to their use; but that was at once apparent when they were taken in conjunction with the hollowed stones. They were corn-crushers, which were used for pounding the parched corn or raw grain to make a thick gruel or porridge.

Later on they improved upon them by using mealing-stones, which ground out the meal by rubbing one stone on another, accompanied with pressure. The stones are in the British Museum. Such mealing-stones were used by the Egyptians and Assyrians, as we shall see, and are employed to this day in Central Africa. 'The mill consists of a block of granite, syenite, or even mica schist, 15in. or 18in. square and five or six thick, with a piece of quartz or other hard rock about the size of a half-brick, one side of which has a convex surface, and fits into a concave hollow in the larger, and stationary, stone. The workwoman, kneeling, grasps this upper

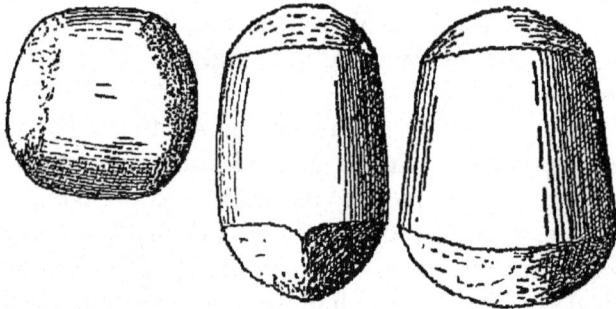

PRE-HISTORIC MILLS AND CORN-CRUSHERS.

C

The History of Bread

millstone with both hands, and works it backwards and forwards in the hollow of the lower millstone, in the same way that a baker works his dough, when pressing it and pushing from him. The weight of the person is brought to bear on the movable stone, and while it is pressed and pushed forwards and backwards one hand supplies, every now and then, a little grain, to be thus at first bruised, and then ground on the lower stone, which is placed on the slope, so that the meal, when ground, falls on to a skin or mat spread for the purpose. This is, perhaps, the most primitive form of mill, and anterior to that in Oriental countries, where two women grind at one mill, and may have been that used by Sarah of old when she entertained the angels.' [1]

To these mealing-stones succeeded the quern. This was a basin, or hollowed stone, with another—oviform—for grinding. The quern has survived to this day. In London, at the west end of Cheapside, by Paternoster Row, was a church, destroyed by the Great Fire of 1666, and never rebuilt, called St. Michael le Quern. It was close by Panyer Alley, so called from the baker's basket, and a stone is still in the alley on which is sculptured a naked boy sitting on a panyer. Querns have been found in the remains of the lake dwellings in Switzerland, and in the Crannoges, or lake dwellings of Scotland and Ireland. They are still in use in out-of-the-way places in Norway, in remote districts in Ireland, and some parts of the western islands of Scotland. In the latter

[1] *Narrative of an Expedition to the Zambesi and its Tributaries*, by David Livingstone. Lond. 1865, p. 543.

Pre-Historic Bread

country, as early as 1284, an effort was made by the Legislature to supersede the quern by the water-mill, the use of the former being prohibited, except in case of storm, or where there was a lack of mills of the new species. Whoever used the quern was to 'gif the threttein measure as multer[1];' and the transgressor was to 'time[2] his hand mylnes perpetuallie.' Querns were not always made of stone, for one made of oak was found in 1831, whilst removing Blair Drummond Moss. It is 19 in. in height by 14 in. in diameter, and the centre is hollowed about a foot, so as to form a mortar.

To sum up this notice of pre-historic bread, I may mention that at Robenhausen, Meisskomer discovered 8lbs. weight of bread, and also at Wangen has been found baked bread or cake made of crushed corn exactly similar. Of course, it has been burnt, or charred, and thus these interesting specimens have been preserved to the present day. The form of these cakes is somewhat round, and about an inch to an inch and a half thick; one small specimen, nearly perfect, is about four or five inches in diameter. The dough did not consist of meal, but of grains of corn more or less crushed. In some specimens the halves of grains of barley are plainly discernible. The under side of these cakes is sometimes flat, sometimes concave, and there appears no doubt that the mass of dough was baked by being laid on hot stones, and covered over with glowing ashes.

[1] Mulcture—fine.   [2] Lose.

CHAPTER II.

THE ancient Egyptians had as cereals three kinds of wheat—*Triticum sativa, zea* and *spelta*; barley, *Hordeum vulgare*, and doura, *Holcus sorghum*, specimens of which may be seen in the Egyptian Gallery at the British Museum. The so-called 'mummy-wheat' is a fallacy, as far as its name goes;

EGYPTIAN REAPERS.

it is the *Triticum turgidum compositum*, cultivated in Egypt, Abyssinia, and elsewhere.

In this fertile land the cultivation of corn was very primitive; the sower had his seed in a basket, which he held in his left hand, or suspended it either on his arm or by a strap round his neck, and he threw the seed broadcast with his right hand.

Corn in Egypt and Assyria

According to the paintings in the tombs, he immediately followed the plough, the light earth needing no
further treatment, and the harrow, in any form, was
unknown. Wheat was cut in about five months after
planting, and barley in about four. We have here a
representation of harvesting, showing the reaping,
with the length of stubble left, and its being tied up
into sheaves, or rather bundles. We next see the
bundles being made into pyramidal stacks.

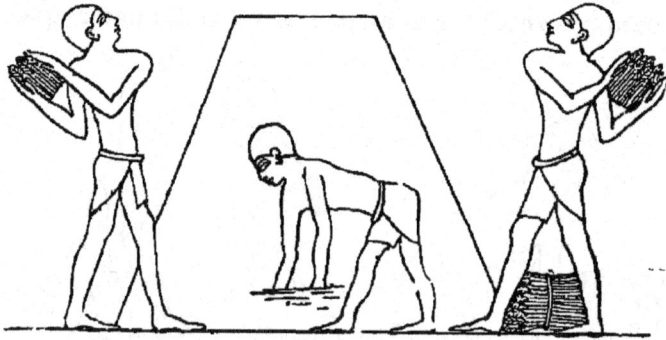

EGYPTIANS STACKING CORN.

Here it remained until it was required for threshing, and then it was transported to the threshing
floor in wicker baskets, upon asses, or in rope nets
borne by two men. These threshing floors were
circular level plots of land, near the field, or in the
vicinity of the granary ; and, the floor being well
swept, the ears were laid down and oxen driven over
it in order to tread out the grain, which was swept up
by an attendant.

And, like their modern brethren, they were merry
at their work and sang songs, several of which may

21

The History of Bread

be seen in the sculptured tombs of Upper Egypt. Champollion gives the following, found in a tomb at Eileithyia:

'Thresh for yourselves (twice repeated),
O oxen,
Thresh for yourselves (twice repeated);
Measures for yourselves,
Measures for your masters.'

Sometimes the cattle were bound by their horns to a piece of wood, which compelled them to move in unison, and tread the corn regularly. But it was also threshed out by manual labour, with curious implements. The next operation was to winnow the corn, which was done with wooden shovels; it was then carried to the granary in sacks, each containing a certain quantity, which was determined by wooden measures, a scribe noting down the number as called by the tellers, who superintended its removal. Herodotus (book II., 14) says that the Egyptians trod out their corn by means of swine.

Besides the growing and gathering of wheat, the doura is also represented in paintings in tombs at Thebes, Eileithyia, Beni-Hassan, and Saggára. Both it and wheat are represented as growing in the same field, but the doura is the taller of the two. It was not reaped, but was pulled up by the roots by men, and sometimes women, who struck off the earth which adhered with their hands, bound it in sheaves, and carried it to a place where it was rippled, as flax is done.

In the ordinary life of the Egyptians, the woman mealed the flour—in as primitive a form as the pre-

EGYPTIANS THRESHING.

EGYPTIANS CARRYING GRAIN TO THE THRESHING FLOOR.

23

The History of Bread

historic man—and in the British Museum are two wooden models, which show the first process of converting the cereal into meal ; and then we have two figures of men kneading dough—from the Museum at Ghizeh (formerly at Boulak). The bread itself was both leavened and unleavened—as may be seen by the many examples—round, triangular, and square—in the British Museum, some of which must have been a foot across, and over an inch thick ; the three examples given on page 27 being 5in. in diameter, and ½in. thick ; 7 ditto and ½ ditto ; whilst the ornamented cake is 3½in. in diameter and ¾in. thick.

But there were professional bakers in Egypt, as we see in some of the tomb-pictures. In the Biblical story of Joseph we find that 'the butler of the King of Egypt and his baker had offended their lord the King of Egypt'; and the Rabbi Solomon says their offences were the butler not having perceived a fly in Pharaoh's cup, and the baker having got a stone into the royal bread, so that Pharaoh thought they were conspiring against his life. We know they were put in prison with Joseph, and related their dreams to him. The dream of the Opheh, or chief baker, was that he 'had three white baskets on his head, and in the uppermost basket there was all manner of bake meats for Pharaoh.' The Bible story of Joseph goes on to tell us how, in the years of plenty, he providentially stored up the excess of corn to meet the years of famine, and how the Israelites sent to Egypt for food, and subsequently abode in that land.

Thanks to Assyrian art, and to the enduring qualities of bronze, we are able to see how that

24

EGYPTIAN METHODS OF BREAD-MAKING.

25

The History of Bread

ancient people made their bread (at least in the camp) during the reign of Shalmaneser II., son of Assur-nasir-abli, who began to govern Assyria about the year 860 B.C., and died in 825 B.C. On the bronze bands of the great gates of Balawat are recorded the warlike doings of Shalmaneser II. in detail. In almost every camp that is represented are men depicted as preparing bread against the return of the, of course, victorious soldiery: we see them mealing

the corn, kneading the dough, making it into flat, round cakes, and, finally, piling these up in large heaps ready for the hungry warriors.

These gates were found in the year 1877 by Mr. Hormuzd Rassam, who, whilst excavating for the Trustees of the British Museum on the site of ancient Nineveh, began also excavations at a mound called Balawat, about 15 miles east of Mosul, and nine miles from Nimroud. Having received, as a present,

EGYPTIAN BREAD.

EGYPTIAN CAKE SELLER.

The History of Bread

before his departure for the East, some fragments of chased bronze, said to have been found in this mound, he naturally had the greatest wish to follow up the indication of a new store of antiquities. He experienced some difficulty from the villagers of Balawat, as the mound had been used by them for some years as a burial ground, and their scruples having been overcome, the result was the finding of these beautiful bronzes in fragments. They were skilfully restored at the British Museum, where they now are, and rank among the best of Assyrian antiquities.

The old Assyrians knew the value of irrigation in growing their crops, and the remains of aqueducts and hydraulic machines which remain in Babylonia bear witness to an advanced civilisation; these are constructed of masonry, which slanted up to the height of two feet, and, disposed at right angles to the river, they conducted the water from 200 to 2000 yards into the interior.

The food of the poor seems to have consisted of grain, such as wheat, or barley, moistened with water, kneaded in a bowl, rolled into cakes and baked in the hot ashes.

CHAPTER III.

BREAD IN PALESTINE.

OF the bread of the ancient Hebrews we know nothing, except from their sacred books; but these contain a large store of knowledge. Their cereals seem to have consisted only of wheat, barley, rye (or it may be spelt), and millet, but they cultivated leguminous plants, such as beans and lentils. It is impossible to say accurately when these books were written, so that in the following notices respecting the bread of the Hebrews I take the sequence in which I find them placed in the Bible. It is impossible to do otherwise, as their chronology is such an open question.

⊣ At first, in all probability, the normal course of pre-historic man was followed—wheat and barley grew wild, were first eaten raw, and then parched. Of this latter and primitive method of cooking cereals we have several notices. It was used as a sacrifice, as we see in Leviticus ii. 16: 'And the priest shall burn the memorial of it, part of the beaten corn thereof, and part of the oil thereof, with all the frankincense thereof: it is an offering made by fire unto the Lord.' That parched corn was at that time a food we find in Levit. xxiii. 14: 'And ye shall eat neither bread, nor parched corn, nor green ears, until the selfsame day that ye have brought an offering unto your God.' We next find it as the food of labouring

29

people in Ruth ii. 14, when Boaz 'reached her parched corn, and she did eat, and was sufficed, and left.'

Mention is again made of it in I. Sam. xvii., when Goliath of Gath challenged the men of Israel. Jesse's three sons had followed Saul to the battle, and the anxious father had sent his youngest son David, with provisions for them, and a present to their commander, vv. 17, 18: 'And Jesse said unto David his son, Take now for thy brethren an ephah[1] of this parched corn, and these ten loaves, and run to the camp to thy brethren; and carry these ten cheeses unto the captain of their thousand, and look how thy brethren fare, and take their pledge.' We see, I. Sam. xxv. 18, how Abigail, Nabal's wife, in order to propitiate David, 'made haste, and took 200 loaves, and two bottles of wine, and five sheep ready dressed, and five measures of parched corn, and 100 clusters of raisins, and 200 cakes of figs, and laid them on asses.' The last we hear of parched corn as food is in II. Sam. xvii. 27, 28, when David arrived at Mahanaim. Shobi, Machir, and Barzillai 'brought beds, and basons, and earthen vessels, and wheat, and barley, and flour, and parched corn, and beans, and lentils, and parched pulse.' In England this parching is sometimes applied to peas, and, indeed, there is a saying comparing an extremely lively person 'to a parched pea in a frying pan,' and in America 'pop corn,' or parched maize, is very popular.

Threshing corn we first read of in Deut. xxv. 4, when we find the following direction given: 'Thou shalt not muzzle the ox when he treadeth out the

---

[1] A measure containing 10 homers, or about 60 pints.

Bread in Palestine

corn,' a practice which the natives of Aleppo, and some other Eastern places, still religiously observe.

How Gideon (Jud. vi. 11) or Ornan (I. Chron. xxi. 20) threshed, whether by oxen or by flail, we cannot tell, but in Isaiah xxviii. 27, 28, we find five methods of threshing then in vogue. 'For the fitches [this is supposed to be the *Nigella sativa*, whose seeds are used as a condiment, like coriander or caraway] are not threshed with a threshing instrument, neither is a cart wheel turned about upon the cummin; but the fitches are beaten out with a staff, and the cummin with a rod. Bread corn is bruised; because he will not ever be threshing it, nor break it with the wheel of his cart, nor bruise it with his horsemen.' In Lowth on *Isaiah* we find this passage made somewhat clearer :

'The dill is not beaten out with the *corn-drag;*
Nor is the *Wheel of the Wain* made to turn upon
  the cummin.
But the dill is beaten out with *the Staff,*
And the cummin with the *Flail,* but
The bread corn with the *Threshing-Wain;*
And not for ever will he continue thus to thresh it,
Nor vex it with the Wheel of its Wain,
Nor to bruise it with the *Hoofs of his Cattle.*'

The *Staff* and *Flail* were used for that grain that was too tender to be treated in any other method. The *Drag* consisted of a sort of frame of strong planks, made rough at the bottom with hard stones or iron ; it was drawn by horses or oxen over the corn sheaves spread on the threshing floor, the driver sitting upon it. The *Wain* was much like the former,

31

but had wheels with iron teeth, or edges like a saw; the axle was armed with iron teeth or serrated wheels throughout; it moved upon three rollers, armed with iron teeth, or wheels, to cut the straw. In Syria they make use of the drag constructed in the very same manner—and this not only forces out the grain, but cuts the straw in pieces for fodder for the cattle; for in Eastern countries there is no hay.

Sir R. K. Porter, in his *Travels in Georgia*,[1] speaks of this method of threshing, which he saw in the early part of the last century. 'The threshing operation is managed by a machine composed of a large square frame of wood, which contains two wooden cylinders placed parallel to each other, and which have a turning motion. They are stuck full of splinters, with sharp square points, but not all of a length. These barrels have the appearance of the barrels in an organ, and their projections, when brought in contact with the corn, break the stalk and disengage the ear. They are put in motion by a couple of cows or oxen, yoked to the frame, and guided by a man sitting on the plank that covers the frame which contains the cylinders. He drives this agricultural equipage in a circle round any great accumulation of just-gathered harvest, keeping at a certain distance from the verge of the heap, close to which a second peasant stands, holding a long-handled 20-pronged fork, shaped like the spread sticks of a fan, and with which he throws the unbound sheaves forward to meet the rotary motion of the machine. He has a shovel also ready, with which he removes to

[1] Vol. II., 89.

Bread in Palestine

a considerable distance the corn that has already passed the wheel. Other men are on the spot with the like implement, which they fill with the broken material, and throw it aloft in the air, where the wind blows away the chaff, and the grain falls to the ground. The latter process is repeated till the corn is completely winnowed from its refuse, when it is gathered up, carried home, and deposited for use in large earthen jars. The straw is preserved with care, being the sole winter food of the horses and mules. But while I looked on at the patriarchal style of husbandry, and at the strong yet docile animal, which for so many ages had been the right hand of man in his business of tilling and reaping the ground, I could not but revere the beneficent law which pronounced, "Muzzle not the ox when he treadeth out the corn."'

It was probably one of these that Araunah meant (II. Sam. xxiv. 22) when he said unto David: 'Let my lord the king take and offer up what seemeth good unto him: behold, here be oxen for burnt sacrifice, and threshing instruments and other instruments of the oxen for wood.' And it is certainly mentioned in Isaiah xli. 15: 'Behold, I will make thee a new sharp threshing instrument having teeth.'

The threshing-floor is many times mentioned in the Bible. There were those of Atad, Nachon, and Araunah (or Ornan), the value of whose floor, etc., is variously stated in II. Sam. xxiv. 24, where it says that David bought the flour and oxen for 50 shekels of silver, or about 6*l* of our money; whilst in I. Chron. xxi. 25, he gave him 600 shekels of gold in weight, or 1200*l* of our currency, which seems a large sum for a small level piece of ground; for the floors, so-called, were out of doors, so that the wind might carry away the chaff, as we read in Hosea xiii. 3: 'They shall be . . . . as the chaff that is driven with the whirlwind out of the floor.' See also Psalm i. 4.

These floors were used for other purposes than threshings, as we read in I. Kings xxii. 10: 'And the king of Israel and Jehoshaphat the king of Judah sat each on his throne, having put on their robes, in a void place (or floor) in the entrance of the gate of Samaria; and all the prophets prophesied before them,' a statement which is repeated in II. Chron. xviii. 9.

Harvest-time was appointed by Moses as one of the great festivals—Exodus xxiii. 14, etc.: 'Three times thou shalt keep a feast unto me in the year. Thou shalt keep the feast of unleavened bread: (thou shalt eat unleavened bread seven days, as I commanded thee, in the time appointed of the month Abib; for in it thou camest out from Egypt: and none shall appear before me empty). And the feast of harvest, the first-fruits of thy labours, which thou hast sown in the field: and the feast of ingathering, which is in the end of the year, when thou hast gathered in thy labours out of the field.' And again, in Exodus xxxiv., this is repeated, with the addition (v. 21): 'Six days thou shalt work, but on the seventh day thou shalt rest: in earing time and in harvest thou shalt rest.' This holiday was, and is, called the feast of tabernacles, and we read in Deut. xvi. 13, etc.: 'Thou shalt observe the feast of tabernacles seven

Bread in Palestine

days, after that thou hast gathered in thy corn and thy wine: and thou shalt rejoice in thy feast, thou, and thy son, and thy daughter, and thy man-servant, and thy maid-servant, and the Levite, the stranger, and the fatherless, and the widow, that are within thy gates. Seven days shalt thou keep a solemn feast unto the Lord thy God in the place which the Lord shall choose: because the Lord thy God shall bless thee in all thine increase, and in all the works of thine hands, therefore thou shalt surely rejoice.'

In the story of Ruth we get an idyllic picture of a Hebrew harvest field, with its kindly greetings between master and man, and its gleaners. Naomi, a native of Bethlehem, returned thither from Moab, after the death of her husband, Elimelech, accompanied by her daughter-in-law Ruth, who was also a widow, 'and they came to Bethlehem in the beginning of barley harvest.'

Special favour was accorded to Ruth. She might glean 'among the sheaves'—*i.e.*, following the reapers, instead of waiting until the corn had been carried ; but the Jews were enjoined to be liberal in the matter of gleaning, as we see by Lev. xix. 9: 'And when ye reap the harvest of your land, thou shalt not wholly reap the corners of thy field, neither shalt thou gather the gleanings of thy harvest'; and in Deut. xxiv. 19, 'When thou cuttest down thine harvest in thy field, and hast forgot a sheaf in the field, thou shalt not go again to fetch it ; it shall be for the stranger, for the fatherless, and for the widow: that the Lord thy God may bless thee in all the work of thine hands.'

There were no public mills at which flour could be

The History of Bread

ground, but, as now, in the unchangeable East, every family ground their own corn, and this task, as well as the making and baking of bread, was left to the women. See Matt. xxiv. 41 : 'Two women shall be grinding at the mill ; the one shall be taken, and the other left.' Again we find that it was a woman who was grinding corn on a housetop in Thebez who (Judges ix. 53) 'cast a piece of a millstone upon Abimelech's head, and all to brake his skull.' An Eastern flour mill consists of two stones, the upper one rotating on the lower. In Shaw's *Travels*, p. 297, he says : ' Most families grind their wheat and barley

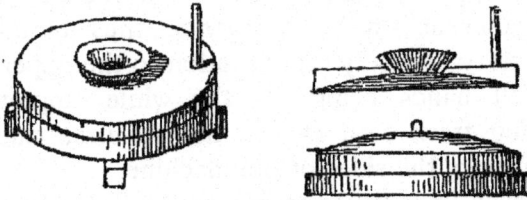

A PALESTINE HAND-MILL.

at home, having two portable millstones for that purpose. The uppermost is turned round by a small handle of wood or iron placed in the edge of it. When this stone is large, or expedition is required, then a second person is called in to assist. It is usual for the women alone to be concerned in this employ, setting themselves down over against each other, with the millstones between them.'

And Dr. Clarke, in his *Travels*,[1] says, that at Nazareth: 'Scarcely had we reached the apartment prepared for our reception, when, looking into the

[1] Vol. IV., 167, 168.

Bread in Palestine

courtyard belonging to the house, we beheld *two women* grinding at the mill in a manner most forcibly illustrating the saying of our Saviour. They were preparing flour to make our bread, as it is always customary in the country when strangers arrive. The two women, seated upon the ground opposite to each other, held between them two round, flat stones, such as are seen in Lapland, and such as in Scotland are called querns. In the centre of the upper stone was a cavity for pouring in the corn, and by the side of this an upright wooden handle for moving the stone. As the operation began, one of the women with her right hand pushed this handle to the woman opposite, who again sent it to her companion, thus communicating a rotary and very rapid motion to the upper stone, their left hands being all the while employed in supplying fresh corn as fast as the bran and flour escaped from the sides of the machine.'

Of such importance among the household treasures of the Hebrews was the flour mill esteemed that Moses laid it down. (Deut. xxiv. 6): 'No man shall take the nether or the upper millstone to pledge: for he taketh a man's life to pledge.'

The first mention of bread in the Bible, with the exception of Adam's curse, is in Gen. xiv. 18: 'And Melchizedek, King of Salem, brought forth bread and wine'; but it is pre-supposed, in Chap. xii. 10: 'And there was a famine in the land: and Abram went down into Egypt to sojourn there; for the famine was grievous in the land.' When the three angels visited him on the plains of Mamre, he offered them hospitality (Gen. xviii. 5, 6): 'I will fetch a morsel

The History of Bread

of bread, and comfort ye your hearts; after that ye shall pass on: for therefore are ye come to your servant. And they said, So do, as thou hast said. And Abraham hastened into the tent unto Sarah, and said, Make ready quickly three measures of fine meal, knead it, and make cakes upon the hearth.' And to this day in Syria cakes are made upon the hearth, and the breaking of bread together is a token of amity and protection extended by the stronger to the weaker.

Of what shape the Hebrew bread was we do not know, for no representation of it has come down to us. As a rule it was possibly in the form of thin flat round cakes—similar to those unleavened biscuits now used by the Jews during their Passover, and the form and dimensions of which are probably traditional—but they also had *loaves* of bread, as we read in many places. The Shew, or Presence bread, must have been loaves, because of the quantity of flour in each —between five and six pints. The directions for making it, etc., are plain enough (Lev. xxiv. 5–9): 'And thou shalt take fine flour, and bake twelve cakes thereof: two tenth deals shall be in one cake. And thou shalt set them in two rows, six on a row, upon the pure table before the Lord. And thou shalt put pure frankincense upon each row, that it may be on the bread for a memorial, even an offering made by fire unto the Lord. Every Sabbath he shall set it in order before the Lord continually, being taken from the children of Israel by an everlasting covenant. And it shall be Aaron's and his sons'; and they shall eat it in the holy place: for it is most holy unto him

Bread in Palestine

of the offerings of the Lord made by fire by a perpetual statute.'

This shew bread must have been leavened, for a cake containing nearly three quarts of flour, and un-leavened, could hardly be. We have no certainty as to the shape of these twelve loaves, typical of the tribes of Israel ; for, although the gold table on which it was placed figures in a *bas relief* on the Arch of Titus at Rome, there is no bread upon it. The Rabbis say that the loaves were square, and covered with leaves of gold ; and that they were placed in two piles of six each, one upon another, on the opposite ends of the table ; and that between every two loaves were laid three semi-tubes, like slit canes, of gold, for the purpose of keeping the cakes the better from mouldiness and corruption by admitting the air between them ; and it is also said, but upon what authority I know not, that each end of the table was furnished with a tall, three-pronged fork of gold, one at each corner, standing perpendicularly, for the purpose of keeping the loaves in their proper places.

The new bread was set on the table with much ceremony every Sabbath, and it was so ordered that the new bread should be set on one end of the table before the old was taken away from the other, in order that the table might not be for a moment without bread. Jewish tradition states that, to render the bread more peculiar and consecrated from its origin, the priests themselves performed all the operations of sowing, reaping and grinding the corn for the shew bread, as well as of kneading and baking the bread itself. On the table was, probably, some salt, as we read in Lev. ii. 13: 'With all thine offerings thou shalt offer salt.'

There seems to be little doubt but that the Israelites knew nothing about leavened bread until they went into Egypt, and that they obtained that knowledge from the civilised Egyptians. That they did leaven their bread we learn from Exodus xii. 34–39: 'And the people took their dough before it was leavened, their kneading-troughs being bound up in their clothes upon their shoulders. . . . . . And they baked unleavened cakes of the dough which they brought forth out of Egypt, for it was not leavened; because they were thrust out of Egypt, and could not tarry, neither had they prepared for themselves any victual.'

Bread was sometimes dipped in oil as a relish, and in this state it was also used in sacrifice. Lev. viii. 26: 'And out of the basket of unleavened bread, that was before the Lord, he took one unleavened cake, and a cake of oiled bread, and one wafer,' etc.; and, occasionally, as we see in Ruth, it was dipped in vinegar. The Jew thanked God for all His good gifts, and with his bread, he took it in his hands, and pronounced the following benediction: 'Blessed art Thou, O Lord our God, the King of the world, that produceth bread out of the earth.' If there were many at table, one asked a blessing for the rest. The blessing always preceded the breaking of the bread. The rules concerning the breaking of bread were— the master of the house recited and finished the blessing, and after that he broke the bread; he did not break a small piece, lest he should seem to be

Bread in Palestine

sparing ; nor a large piece, lest he should be thought
to be famished ; it was a principal command to
break a whole loaf. He that broke the bread put a
piece before everyone, and the other took it into his
hand. The master of the family ate first of the bread
after blessing. Maimonides, writing on *Halacoth*, or
legal formulæ (*Beracoth*, c. 7), says the guests were
not to eat or taste anything till he who broke had
tasted first, nor was it permitted at festivals for any
of the guests to drink of the cup till the master of the
family had done so.

There are several unleavened bread bakeries in
London, and one each in Birmingham and Leeds, to
supply the Jews resident in the neighbourhood with
Passover cakes, or *Matzos*. Of course, there is an
enormous demand for this sort of unleavened bread,
and to meet it these bakeries begin baking two
months before the commencement of the Passover.
These *Matzos* look like ordinary large water biscuits,
except that they are a foot or more in diameter.
They are made of flour and water, and contain no
other ingredient.

After the flour has been kneaded into a very stiff
dough, a lump of it, weighing about 50 lb., is placed
on a great block of wood and pressed into a thick
sheet by a heavy beam, which is fastened to the block
at one end by an iron link and staple. This sheet is
next placed under an iron roller, from which it
emerges in a long ribbon. It passes under another
roller, and another, and then it is thin enough for
baking. It is now stamped and cut into the unbaked
Matzos, which are placed upon a large peel, or wooden

The History of Bread

tray, having a long handle, and deposited in an oven. Three minutes later they are taken out, white, but crisp. From the oven they are conveyed to the packing room, where they are allowed to cool, after which they are put up in stacks, and thus kept ready for delivery. Of course, during the whole of Passover week the Jews eat no other bread.

CHAPTER IV.

THE BREAD OF THE CLASSIC LANDS.

As an introduction to the bread of the Romans and Greeks, let us begin with the pretty myth of Demeter (or Ceres, as the Romans called her), and her daughter Persephone. Zeus, or Jupiter, had promised his daughter Persephone to Pluto, without informing Demeter of his plan, and whilst the girl was plucking flowers which Zeus had caused to grow, in order to fix her attention, Pluto seized her, and, the earth opening, they disappeared, and went to his kingdom of Hades. Many places have been assigned as the spot where this took place; but the ancient Eleusis, not far from Salamis or Athens, now the little village of Lefsina, has, if such a thing were possible, perhaps the prior claim, for here stood the famous temple of Demeter, now lately (1882–89) excavated and surveyed, and here were performed the Eleusinian mysteries in her honour.

The shrieks of Persephone were heard only by Hecate and Helios; and her mother, hearing only the echo of her voice, at once darted down to earth in search of her beloved child. Hopelessly and aimlessly she wandered about, caring nothing for herself; and for nine whole days and nights neither eat nor drank, tasted neither nectar nor ambrosia, nor did she even bathe herself. On the tenth day she met Hecate, who

43

The History of Bread

told her all she knew of her daughter's disappearance, which was not much, as she had heard but her piercing cries. But, thinking that Helios, the all-seeing sun, might have viewed the scene, they hastened to him, and he told them how it all happened: how Pluto had carried off her daughter, with the approval and consent of Zeus.

Heart-broken at this conduct of the father of her child, she would have no more of the society of the gods, and forswore Olympus, preferring to live rather among men on earth. And so she dwelt among them, rewarding those who were kind to her and severely punishing those who did not treat her well; and in this way, still wandering and mourning for her lost child, she came to Eleusis, where Celeus was king.

But her wrath was still as fierce as ever, and, by withholding her gifts, the fields produced no crops, and there was famine upon earth, and so sore indeed did it become that Zeus, perceiving it, feared that the race of man might become extinct for lack of food, and sent Iris as ambassador to try and persuade Demeter to return to Olympus. But she was firm, although all the gods were sent to her to induce her to relent, and nothing would she do to mitigate the evil she had wrought, save on the condition that her daughter should be restored to her.

Hermes was sent to Pluto, and his mission met with partial success. Persephone had eaten of the pomegranate seed, which sacredly pledged her to her dread lord; and for three months in the year she must leave her mother and the fair earth and go to

The Bread of the Classic Lands

live in Pluto's dreary kingdom. Hermes fulfilled his mission by restoring her to her loving mother, who rejoiced over her with an exceeding joy. Zeus, choosing this happy moment, sent Rhea to Demeter to conciliate her and prevail upon her to return to Olympus—a task which she happily effected. The earth smiled once more and became fertile, and

THE LEGEND OF DEMETER AND TRIPTOLEMUS.

Demeter, with her daughter, to whom she was lent for nine months in the year, went to dwell once more in the companionship of the gods; but, before she left the earth, she rewarded Celeus, the King of Eleusis, who had been kind to her, by giving his son, Triptolemus, a chariot with winged dragons and seeds of wheat. His chariot was useful, for by means of it he was able to ride all over the earth, and

45

The History of Bread

instruct men in growing corn. He established the worship of Demeter at Eleusis, and instituted the mysteries in honour of the goddess.

And in this pretty myth of Demeter and Persephone we may trace the story of the seasons; how for nine months the earth is smiling and fertile, and for the remaining three is dead.

Dr. Schliemann claimed to have found the site of ancient Troy when he uncovered the hill of Hissarlik. It was undoubtedly the remains of a pre-historic city, and one which had advanced to a considerable amount of civilisation. And this is shown particularly in one instance, in the huge earthenware jars, or *pithoi*, that were used for storing corn and wine. The following illustration gives a graphic description of them as they appeared *in situ*: 'One of the compartments of the uppermost houses below the Temple of Athené, and belonging to the third, the burnt city, appears to have been used as a magazine for storing corn or wine, for there are in it nine enormous earthenware jars of various forms, about 5 ft. high and $4\frac{3}{4}$ ft. across, their mouths being from $29\frac{1}{2}$ in. to $35\frac{1}{4}$ in. broad. Each of them has four handles $3\frac{3}{4}$ in. broad, and the clay of which they are made is as much as $2\frac{1}{4}$ in. thick.'[1]

Dr. Schliemann says [p. 279]: 'The number of large jars which I brought to light in the burnt stratum of the third city certainly exceeds 600. By far the larger number of them were empty, the mouth being covered by a large flag of schist or limestone. This leads me to the conclusion that the jars were

[1] *Ilios.* By Dr. H. Schliemann. London, 1880, pp. 32, 33.

The Bread of the Classic Lands

filled with wine or water at the time of the catastrophe, for there appears to have been hardly any reason for covering them if they had been empty. Had they been used to contain anything else but liquids, I should have found traces of the fact, but only in a very few cases did I *find some carbonised grain* in the jars, and only twice a small quantity of a white mass, the nature of which I could not determine.'

PITHOI FOUND AT HISSARLIK.

So that we see that this pre-historic nation not only grew corn, but stored it for future use.

The means this pre-historic people had of crushing or mealing the grain was the same as usual : the saddle querns, or two stones with flat surfaces, between which the grain was crushed and roughly triturated—so frequently found on the Continent, and the pestle and mortar of the lake dwellings, as also round stones for fitting into hollows such as are found in the lakes, the cave dwellings of the Dordogne and in the

47

The History of Bread

dolmens of France. Dr. Schliemann, in describing 'the Trojan saddle querns,' says they 'are either of trachyte or of basaltic lava, but by far the larger number are of the former material. They are of oval form, flat on one side and convex on the other, and resemble an egg cut longitudinally through the middle. Their length is from 7 in. to 14 in., and even as much as 25 in.; the very long ones are generally crooked longitudinally, their breadth is from 5 in. to 14 in. The grain was bruised between the flat sides of two of these querns; but only a kind of groats can have been produced in this way, not flour. The bruised grain could not have been used for making bread. In *Homer* we find it used for porridge (*Il.* xviii., 558–560), and also for strewing on the roasted meat (*Od.* xiv., 76–77).'

In Homeric times the corn was evidently ground by millstones (which were, probably, precisely similar to those found by Dr. Schliemann), as we see in *Il.* vii. 270, xii., 161, and *Od.* vii., 104, xx., 105. Pliny N.H., xxxvi., 30, speaking of millstones says: 'In no country are the molar stones superior to those of Italy; stones, be it remembered, not fragments of rock; there are some provinces, too, where they are not to be found at all. Some stones of this class are softer than others, and admit of being smoothed with the whetstone, so as to present all the appearance, at a distance, of serpentine. There is no more durable stone than this; for, in general, stone, like wood, suffers from the action, more or less, of rain, heat, and cold. . . . Some persons give this molar stone the

48

The Bread of the Classic Lands

name of *pyrites*, from the circumstance that it has a great affinity to fire.'

In book xviii., 23, Pliny gives us *the mode of grinding corn*. 'All the grains are not easily broken. In Etruria they first parch the spelt in the ear, and then pound it with a pestle shod with iron at the end. In this instrument the iron is notched at the bottom, sharp ridges running out like the edge of a knife, and concentrating in the form of a star, so that, if care is

POUNDING GRAIN.

not taken to hold the pestle perpendicularly while pounding, the grains will only be splintered and the iron teeth broken. Throughout the greater part of Italy, however, they employ a pestle that is only rough at the end, and wheels turned by water, by means of which the corn is gradually ground. I shall here set forth the opinions given by Mago as to the

The History of Bread

best method of pounding corn. He says that the wheat should be steeped first of all in water, and then cleaned from the husk, after which it should be dried in the sun and then pounded with the pestle ; the same plan, he says, should be adopted in the preparation of barley.'

This was how corn was prepared in some parts of Italy at the time of the Christian era, by the same method as that described by Livingstone : 'The corn is pounded in a large wooden mortar, like the ancient Egyptian one, with a pestle six feet long and about four inches thick. The pounding is performed by two or even three women at one mortar. Each, before delivering a blow with her pestle, gives an upward jerk of the body, so as to put strength into the stroke, and they keep exact time, so that two pestles are never in the mortar at the same moment. . . . By the operation of pounding, with the aid of a little water, the hard outside scale or husk of the grain is removed, and the corn is made fit for the millstone. The meal irritates the stomach unless cleared from the husk ; without considerable energy in the operation the husk sticks fast to the corn. Solomon thought that still more vigour than is required to separate the hard husk or bran from the wheat would fail to separate "a fool from his folly." "Though thou shouldest bray a fool in a mortar among wheat with a pestle, yet will not his foolishness depart from him." '

We have noticed the primitive Homeric mill-stones and the Etruscan pestles and mortars, but at the time of the Christian era things molinary were

The Bread of the Classic Lands

somewhat more advanced. Doubtless in parts of the country the hand mill or quern, called *Mola manuaria*, *versatilis* or *trusatilis*, was in use, and it was worked

A BAKEHOUSE AT POMPEII.

by slaves, who were sent to the *pistorineum* as a punishment. But the usual corn mill was worked by

The History of Bread

animals, and was called *Mola iumentaria* or *Mola asinaria.*

Both Greeks and Romans originally ground their flour and baked their bread at home, and mills and bakeries have been found in several private houses in Pompeii. One of these bakeries was attached to the house of Sallust, on the south side, being divided from it only by a narrow street. Its front is the main street, or Via Consularis, leading from the gate of Herculaneum to the Forum. Entering by a small vestibule, the visitor finds himself in a portico of ample dimensions, considering the character of the house, being about 36 feet by 30 feet. At the end of the portico is an opening through which the bakehouse is entered, which is at the back of the house, and opens into a smaller street, which, diverging from the main street at the fountain by Pansa's house, runs straight up to the city walls. The work room of the mill and bakery is about 33 feet long by 26 feet. The centre is occupied by four stone mills, and when it was uncovered, the ironwork, though entirely rust eaten, was yet perfect enough to explain satisfactorily the method of construction.

Not only were the flour mills, kneading troughs and other utensils for baking found in Pompeii, but there were also loaves of bread, of round form, and sub-divided, some of which were stamped with the baker's name. That this was the usual form of loaf is also shown by a painting on the walls of the Temple of Augustus, where we see the bread partially broken, and by the representation of a baker's shop, where all the loaves are similarly shaped.

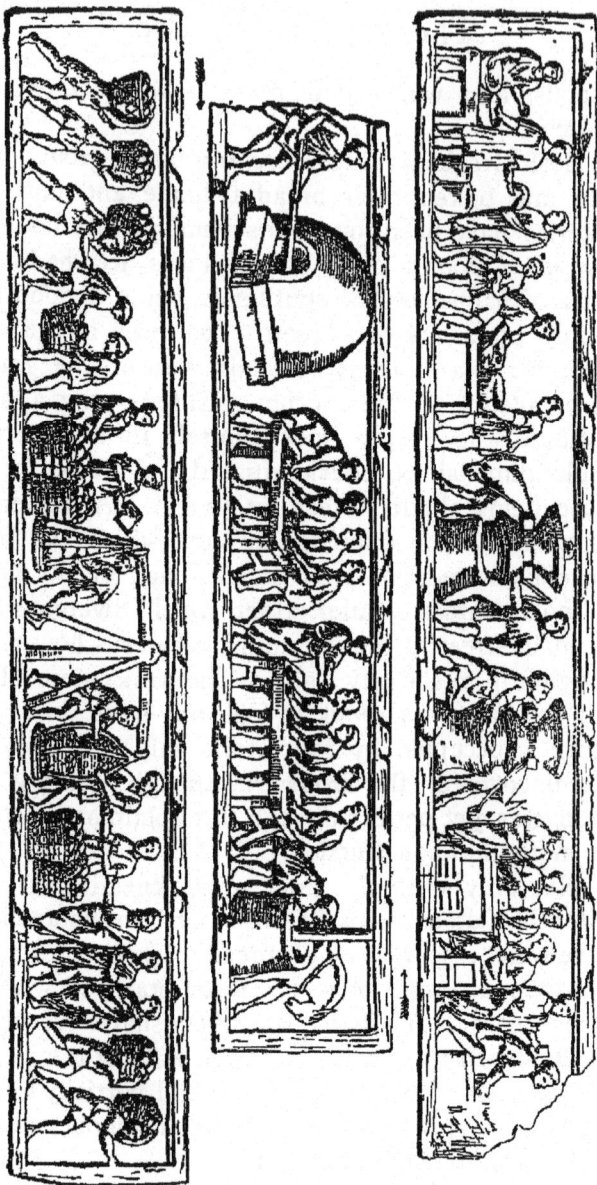

ROMAN METHODS OF BREAD-MAKING.

The History of Bread

This, at all events, seems to have been the shape in vogue about the time of the Christian era ; but in the *bas reliefs* on the tomb of Eurysaces, who was a baker in a large way of business at Rome, they seem to be globular. These *bas reliefs* are most interesting, as they show the whole history of baking. First there

A BAKER'S SHOP AT POMPEII.

is the purchase of the corn, and payment being made for it ; then we see it ground, and sifted to separate the bran. Next a man is buying some flour. Then we see the dough being kneaded by horse-power, the bakers making it into loaves, the baker with his peel baking the loaves, which are afterwards carried in

The Bread of the Classic Lands

paniers to be weighed. Then there are the customers, and the bread being sent out for delivery.

Pliny tells us that there were no bakers at Rome until the war with King Perseus of Macedon, more than 580 years after the building of the city. The ancient Romans used to make their own bread, it being an occupation which belonged to the women, as we see is the case in many nations even at the present day. In those times they had no cooks in the number of their slaves, but used to hire them for the occasion from the market. The Gauls were the first to employ the bolter that is made of horse-hair ; while the people of Spain made their sieves and meal dressers of flax, and the Egyptians of papyrus and rushes.

Many freedmen were engaged as bakers, and under the Republic it was one of the duties of the œdiles to see that the bread was properly prepared and correct in weight. Grain was delivered into public granaries by enrolled *Saccarii*, and it was distributed to the bakers by a corporation called the *Catabolenses*. A bakers' guild (*corpus* or *collegium pistorum*), which long existed, was organised by Trajan, and this body, through its connection with the *cura amonæ*, became of much importance, and enjoyed various privileges. There were guilds of *pistores* and *clibanarii* at Pompeii. A great increase in the number of bakeries (*pistrinæ, officinæ pistoriæ*) afterwards took place at Rome, owing, probably, to the action of Aurelian in introducing a daily distribution of bread, instead of the old monthly distribution of grain that had been usual since the time of Gracchi.

CHAPTER V.

BREAD IN EASTERN LANDS.

AGRICULTURE has always taken a prominent part in Chinese polity, and is incorporated in their religious observances; and a deep veneration for it is inscribed on all the institutions in China. Among the several grades of society the cultivators of mind rank first, then those of land, third come the manufacturers, and lastly the merchants. Homage to agriculture is done annually by the Emperor, who makes a show of performing its operations.

This ceremony, which originated more than 2000 years ago, had been discontinued by degenerate princes, but was revived by Yong-tching, the third of the Mantchoo dynasty. This anniversary takes place on the 24th day of the second moon, coinciding with our month of February. The monarch prepares himself for it by fasting three days; he then repairs to the appointed spot with three princes, nine presidents of the high tribunals, forty old and forty young husbandmen. Having performed a preliminary sacrifice of the fruits of the earth to Shang-ti, the supreme deity, he takes in his hand the plough, and makes a furrow of some length, in which he is followed by the princes and other grandees. A similar course is observed in sowing the field, and the operations are completed by the husbandmen.

Bread in Eastern Lands

An annual festival in honour of Agriculture is also celebrated in the capital of each province. The governor marches forth, crowned with flowers, and accompanied by a numerous train, bearing flags adorned with agricultural emblems and portraits of eminent husbandmen, while the streets are decorated with lanterns and triumphal arches.

Although rice is the staple grain in use in China, wheat-growing is one of the principal industries in the northern and middle parts of that country. The winter wheat is planted at about the same time that wheat is planted here. The soil, especially in the northern provinces, is so well worn that it is unfitted for wheat-growing, and the Chinese farmers, appreciating this fact, and the fact that all kinds of fertilisers are excessively dear, make the least money do the most good by mixing the seed with finely-prepared manure.

A man with a basket swung upon his shoulders follows the plough, and plants the mixture in large handsful in the furrows, so that when the crop grows up it looks like young celery. Immediately after the first melting of snow, and when the ground has become sufficiently hardened by frost, these wheat-fields are turned into pastures, under the theory that, by a timely clipping of the tops of these plants, the crops will grow up with additional strength in the spring.

Wheat-threshing is the principal interest in Chinese farming. Owing to the scarcity of fuel, the wheat is usually pulled up by the root, bundled in sheaves, and carted to the *mien-chong*, a smooth and hardened

The History of Bread

space of ground near the home of the farmer. The top of the sheaves is then clipped off by a hand machine. The wheat is then left in the *mien-chong* to dry, whilst the headless sheaves are piled in a heap for fuel or thatching. When the wheat is thoroughly dry it is beaten under a great stone roller pulled by horses, while the places thus rolled are constantly tossed over with pitchforks. The stalks left untouched by the roller are threshed with flails by women and boys. The beaten stalks and straws are then taken out by an ingenious arrangement of pitchforks, and the chaff is removed by a systematic tossing of the grain into the air until the wind blows every particle of chaff or dust out of the wheat. Even the chaff is carefully swept up and stowed away for fuel or other useful purposes, such as stuffing mattresses or pillows. After the wheat is allowed to dry for a few hours in the burning sun, it is stowed away in airy bamboo bins.

The milling process is a very ancient one. Two large round bluestone wheels, with grooves neatly cut in the faces on one side, and in the centre of the lower wheel a solid wooden plug is used. The process of making flour out of wheat by this machinery is called *mob-mien*. Usually a horse or mule is employed; the poor, having no animals, grind the grain themselves.

Three distinct qualities of flour are thus produced. The *shon-mien*, or A grade, is the first siftings ; the *nee-mien*, or second grade, is the grindings of the rough leavings from the first siftings, which is of a darker and redder colour than the first grade ; and *mod* is the finely-ground last siftings of all grades.

Bread in Eastern Lands

When bread is made from this grade it resembles rough gingerbread. This is usually the food of the poorest families. The bread of the Chinese is usually fermented, and then steamed. Only a very small quantity is baked in ovens. But the staple articles of food in Northern China are wheat, millet, and sweet potatoes. Wheat and rice are the food of the rich, while the middle classes of the Empire eat millet

CHINESE METHOD OF HUSKING GRAIN.

and rice. In the southern provinces the entire bread-stuff is rice.

At King-Kiang wheat is served as rice. It is first threshed with flails made of bamboo, and then pounded by a rough stone hammer, working in a mortar which rests on a pivot, and is operated like a treadle by the human foot. This separates the husks, and it is then winnowed, the grain being afterwards ground in the usual way.

The History of Bread

Rice is undoubtedly the staple food of those parts of China where it will grow, in spite of its being a precarious crop, the failure of which means famine. A drought in its early stages withers it, and an inundation, when nearly ripe, is equally destructive; whilst the birds and locusts, which are fearfully numerous in China, infest it more than any other grain. Rice requires not only intense heat, but moisture so abundant that the field in which it grows must be repeatedly laid under water. These requisites exist only in the districts south of the Yang-tse Kiang (the Yellow River) and its several tributaries. Here a vast extent of land is perfectly fitted for this valuable crop. Confined by powerful dykes, these rivers do not generally, like the Nile, overflow and cover the country; but by means of canals their waters are so widely distributed that almost every farmer, when he pleases, can inundate his field. This supplies not only moisture, but a fertilising mud or slime, washed down from the distant mountains. The cultivator thus dispenses with manure, of which he labours under a great scarcity, and considers it enough if the grain be steeped in liquid manure.

The Chinese always transplant their rice. A small space is enclosed, and very thickly sown, after which a thin sheet of water is led or pumped over it; in the course of a few days the shoots appear, and when they have attained the height of six or seven inches the tops are cut off, and the roots transplanted to a field prepared for the purpose, when they are set in rows about six inches from each other. The whole surface is again supplied with moisture, which continues to cover the plants till they approach maturity, when the ground is allowed to become dry.

The first harvest is reaped in the end of May or beginning of June, the grain being cut with a small sickle, and carried off the field in frames suspended from bamboo poles placed across a man's shoulders. Barrow (p. 565) thus describes one: 'The machine usually employed for clearing rice from the husk, in the large way, is exactly the same as that now used in Egypt for the same purpose, only that the latter is put in motion by oxen and the former commonly by water. This machine consists of a long horizontal axis of wood, with cogs, or projecting pieces of wood or iron, fixed upon it at certain intervals, and it is turned by a water-wheel. At right angles to this axis are fixed as many horizontal levers as there are circular rows of cogs ; these levers act on pivots that are fastened into a low brick wall, but parallel to the axis and at the distance of about two feet from it. At the further extremity of each lever, and perpendicular to it, is fixed a hollow pestle, directly over a large mortar of stone or iron sunk into the ground ; the other extremity extending beyond the wall, being pressed upon by the cogs of the axis in its rotation, elevates the pestle, which by its own gravity falls into the mortar. An axis of this kind sometimes gives motion to 15 or 20 levers.'

Meantime the stubble is burnt on the land, over which the ashes are spread as its only manure ; a second crop is immediately sown, and reaped about the end of October, when the straw is left to putrify

The History of Bread

on the ground, which is allowed to rest till the commencement of the ensuing spring.

As the cereal food of the Chinese is principally boiled rice, it stands to reason that bakers are not numerous, bread only appearing at the tables of high-class mandarins. It is chiefly replaced by fancy biscuits and numberless kinds of pastry, made not only with wheaten flour, but also that of rice—these serve as vehicles for the various jams and fruit *compotes* for which the Chinese are famous, and which they know so well how to make ; in fact, the bakers are more strictly confectioners, and they can be seen any day busy in their shops baking cakes of rice flour and ground almonds of every imaginable shape and varied in quality by spices. Not only so, but these cakes are sold, already baked, in the peripatetic cookeries which go about the streets. Out of wheaten flour they make a kind of vermicelli, which is much esteemed by the Chinese.

Failure of the rice crops, and consequent famine in Japan, have been the means of introducing wheaten flour into this country more rapidly than anything else could have done. Most remarkable is the universal favour that bread and similar floury concoctions are beginning to enjoy in the treaty ports. This article of food has become completely Japanized, and sells in forms unknown to Europeans. *Tsuke-pau*, sold by peripatetic vendors, who push their wares along in a tiny roofed hand-cart, is much liked by the poorer classes. It consists of slices—thick, generous slices—of bread dipped in soy and brown sugar, and then fried or toasted. Each slice has a skewer passed through it, which the buyer returns after demolishing the bread.

Flour is now used in many other ways besides the manufacture of simple bread. There is *Kash-pau*, cake bread, which is sold everywhere. As the name implies, it is a sort of sweet breadstuff made into cakes of various sizes and artistic figures, according to the skill and fancy of the baker. To an European palate this *Kash-pau* is rather dry and tasteless, but it is very cheap, and for five *sen* (three-halfpence) a huge paper bagful can be bought. *Kasuteira*, or sponge cake, is not so much sought after as it used to be. Yet some bakeries, such as the *Fugetsu-do* and *Tsuboya*, excel in producing the lightest and most delicious sponge cake.

Millet, in China, is only used as food by the very poor.

Wheat is not the primary article of food among the natives of India, and hitherto only enough has been produced for home consumption; but of late years much has been grown for export, and being of a particularly hard nature is useful for mixing with the softer kinds. Still, it is used by itself, and is made into unleavened cakes called *Chupatees*. These are made by mixing flour and water together, with a little salt, into a paste or dough, kneading it well; sometimes *ghee* (clarified butter) is added. They may also be made with milk instead of water. They are flattened into thin cakes with the hand, smeared with a small quantity of *ghee*, and baked on an iron pan, or sheet of iron, over the fire.

Historic, too, is the *Chupatee*, for by its means the

The History of Bread

message was sent round throughout the length and breadth of British India for the rising against the English rule—known as the Indian Mutiny. Its true meaning was not at first understood, as we may read in the Indian correspondence of the *Times*, dated Bombay, March 3, 1857 : 'From Cawnpore to Allahabad, and onwards towards the great cities of the North-West, the *chokedars*, or policemen, have been of late spreading from village to village—at whose command, or for what object, they themselves, it is said, are ignorant—little plain cakes of wheaten flour. The number of cakes, and the mode of their transmission, is uniform. *Chokedar* of village A enters village B, and, addressing its *chokedar*, commits to his charge two cakes, with directions to have other two similar to them prepared ; and, leaving the old in his own village, to hie with the new to village C, and so on. English authorities of the districts through which these edibles passed looked at, handled, and probably tasted them ; and finding them, upon the evidence of all their senses, harmless, reported accordingly to the Government. And it appears, I think, with tolerable clearness, that the mysterious mission is not of political but of superstitious origin ; and is directed simply to the warding off of diseases, such as the choleraic visitation of twelve months ago, in which point of view it is noteworthy and characteristic, and not unworthy to be remembered together with last year's grim and picturesque legend of the horseman, who rode down to the river at dead of night and was ferried across, announcing that the pestilence was in his train.'

Bread in Eastern Lands

Apropos of Indian flour, Col. Meadows Taylor, in *The Story of My Life*, tells a story anent the adulteration of flour in India.

'During that day my tent was beset by hundreds of pilgrims and travellers, crying loudly for justice against the flour-sellers, who not only gave short weight in flour, but adulterated it so distressingly with sand that the cakes made with it were uneatable, and had to be thrown away. That evening I told some reliable men of my escort to go quietly into the bazaars and each buy flour at a separate shop, being careful to note whose shop it was.

'The flour was brought to me. I tested every sample, and found it full of sand as I passed it under my teeth. I then desired that all the persons named in my list should be sent to me with their baskets of flour, their weights and scales. Shortly afterwards they arrived, evidently suspecting nothing, and were placed in a row seated on the grass before my tent.

' "Now," said I gravely, "each of you is to weigh out a ser (two pounds) of your flour," which was done. "Is it for the pilgrims?" asked one.

' "No," said I quietly, though I had much difficulty to keep my countenance. "You must eat it yourselves."

'They saw that I was in earnest, and offered to pay any fine that I imposed.

' "Not so," I returned, "you have made many eat your flour; why should you object to eat it yourselves?"

'They were horribly frightened, and, amid the jeers and screams of laughter of the bystanders, some of them actually began to eat, spluttering out the

The History of Bread

half-moistened flour, which could be heard crunching between their teeth. At last some of them flung themselves on their faces, abjectly beseeching pardon.

' "Swear!" I cried, "swear by the Holy Mother in yonder temple that you will not fill the mouths of her worshippers with dirt! You have brought this on yourselves, and there is not a man in all the country who will not laugh at the *bunnais* (flour-sellers) who could not eat their own flour because it broke their teeth."

'So this episode terminated, and I heard no more complaints of bad flour.'

The Indian flour mill is very primitive, consisting of two great mill-stones, of which the lower is fast, and the upper is usually turned by two women, who feed the wheat by handfuls into a hole which passes through the stone. The meal so obtained is simply mixed with palm yeast, and baked in very hot ovens, which have been heated for several days. The small European householder finds it more convenient to patronise the Mohammedan bakers, of whom, however, the bread has to be ordered in advance. Sometimes two or three English families combine, and hire a baker, paying him a monthly salary, and providing him with the raw material.

The yeast mentioned above is made from the sap of the date palm. In April, before the flowers appear, a Hindoo climbs the naked trunk—for the leaves, as in all palm trees, are borne on the top. The man's feet are bound together by a rope, and about his hips are fastened two pots for the reception of the sap. As he climbs, he calls out, '*Darpor, darpor ata hain*,' which, being interpreted, means, 'The palm-tapper is coming.' This is for the benefit of the Mohammedan women who might be sitting unveiled in the court-yards of the houses exposed to the view of the climber after he has risen above the tops of the walls. A tapper who once fails to give this warning cry is thenceforth forbidden to ply his trade. When the tapper has reached the crown of the tree he cuts two gashes in opposite sides of the trunk with an axe, which he has carried up in his mouth. Then he fastens the pots under the gashes and descends. The full pots are taken away and empty ones put in their place twice daily. The sap has a sweet taste, and contains some alcohol even when fresh. After standing in the sun in great earthen pots for a few days it begins to ferment, after which it deposits a thick white substance. This, taken at the proper time, is used as yeast.

But rice is, in India, the staff of life, being used to a greater extent than any grain in Europe. It is, in fact, the food of the highest and the lowest, the principal harvest of every climate. Its production, generally speaking, is only limited by the means of irrigation, which is essential to its growth. The ground is prepared in March and April ; the seed is sown in May and reaped in August. If circumstances are favourable there are other harvests, one between July and November, another between January and April. These also sometimes consist of rice, but more commonly of other grain or pulse. In some parts millet is used as food. Many are the ways of cooking rice—there are powder of cucumber seeds and

The History of Bread

rice, lime juice and rice, orange juice and rice, jack fruit and rice, rice and milk, and sweet cakes made of rice flour, with or without green ginger.

The Bombay baker is a man of a different stamp altogether to the Bengal baker. He is invariably a Goanese and a native Christian, and adopts his profession not from choice but by heredity. For generations past his fathers have been bakers, and have, in accordance with the rules of the Society of Bakers, to which they must have belonged, studied some portion at least of the art of manufacturing bread. The Bombay baker is, moreover, a man of substance. To begin with, he grows his own wheat, and has it conveyed to his factories, where as many as 200 hands are employed in converting it into raw material for cooking. He retains a staff of *chefs*, who also hail from Goa, and who attend exclusively to the baking. Greater comparative intelligence and a love for his trade enable him to turn out a far superior article to that of his ignorant contemporary in Upper India ; but even in Bombay the same fault has to be found with the manufacturer : either the bread is too fine, or it is too 'brown'—that is, it contains too much bran.

CHAPTER VI.

BREAD IN EUROPE AND AMERICA.

OLAUS MAGNUS, Archbishop of Upsala, who lived in the first half of the 16th century, has left behind him, in his *Historia de Gentibus Septentrionalibus,* a long and lucid account of Scandinavian life and manners. Respecting harvest, he tells us that in the Northern countries, in many fields of the Visigoths, on that part that lies southward, barley is ripe and mown in 36 days from the date of sowing—that is, from the end of June to the middle of August, and sometimes sooner ; and other corn sown in the beginning of May is reaped in the middle of August—'by the mutual help of the countrymen, not with any great pains, but with alacrity and willing minds, lest cold wind should blow upon it and blast the corn. And they desire no other reward for their daily labour than a merry feast at night, where the young people of both sexes, by reason of their faithful labours in the field, by the judgment, consent, and permission of their provident parents, are made choice of for to be married.'

He tells us that the farther North you go the less wheat is grown, but there is more towards the South, the Swedes having plenty of wheat but more rye. 'But the Goths, both East and West, who feed on barley and oats, have an infinite abundance given them by the mercy of God. Yet there is use made of all these sorts of corn in both places. But the Swedes provide most of rye, where their women know so well how to winnow rye, that for colour, taste, and for health it surpasses the goodness of wheat.'

In order to preserve their corn they carefully dried it. 'On the hottest days, when the sun shines strong, they spread cloths like ships' sails, or else the sails

EARLY SCANDINAVIAN BAKERIES.

themselves, upon the ground, or on the tops of mountains where there is no grass, and they lay the corn out to dry for six, or more, or fewer days, as the sun shines hot; then when it is cleaned they lay it up in vessels of oak, or else they grind it, and so lay it up safe, and when it is so dried it will last good for years. But if it be not ground meal, but corn, it is convenient once a year to set it in the sun to be again dried, and thus new-dried corn may be mingled with it prudently. But the meal thrust into the oaken vessels, or tuns, by strong ramming it in with wooden mallets, and laid up in a dry place, will last many years, and never be worm-eaten.'

He also discourses on the variety of mills for grinding corn in use. How there was the windmill, that turned by running water, by horse-power, by hands and feet—backwards and forwards, like the

EARLY SCANDINAVIAN BAKERIES.

pre-historic mealing stones, and also the quern; but he mostly extols the windmills of Holland.

The grain being ground, it was ready for making into bread, and he minutely describes the operation —how it was kneaded into a round shape, then rolled very thin, and finally baked on a sheet of iron, like a warrior's shield, supported by a tripod, and heated by a slow fire—in fact, the griddle, or girdle, cakes of North Britain. But there was other bread

The History of Bread

which was baked in an oven ; and here the artist seems to have drawn somewhat upon his imagination for his cockroaches and blackbeetles. It seems that bread was not sold by weight, and that they were in the habit, about Christmas time, of making what we should call dough babies, about the size of a five-year-old child, of which they made presents, and similar, but smaller, babies of wheat-flour, which they sold.

They also made a gingerbread of flour, honey, and spices, which travellers in the winter made use of; another bread of flour, milk, butter, eggs, and ginger. Then, also, they baked biscuits for shipboard and for victualling forts, but he pathetically points out that these biscuits, if kept for a length of time, especially in a damp place, developed dangerous energy in the shape of weevils, which were harmless (*non tamen noxii*). He says of the griddle cakes that they would keep good for twenty or more years, by which time they would be reasonably stale.

Scarcely two centuries have passed since rye flour, by itself, or mixed with wheat, furnished nearly all the bread consumed by the labouring classes of England. With the exception of wheat, rye contains a greater proportion of gluten than any other cereal, to which fact it owes its capability of being converted into a spongy bread ; and if anyone wishes to try it for themselves, here is a recipe for making *Grislex Surbröd* or *Husholdinngsbröd* (bread for the household), which is the ordinary bread for the eastern parts of Norway.

Bread in Europe and America

'Contrary to our expectations we found white bread everywhere, but the common bread is a heavy bread, the chief ingredient of which is rye. It is always sour—the goodwife intends it to be so. They also have "flat bread" (*flad bröd*) made of potatoes and rye. It was this kind of bread that the two women whom we happened in upon were making. They were in a little underground room, unlighted except from the door.

'The women making the bread were seated on either side of a long, low table, upon which were huge mounds of dough. The one nearest the door cut off a piece of this, and moulded it, and rolled it out to a certain degree of thinness; then the other one took it, and, with the greatest care, rolled it still more. At her right hand was the fireplace, and upon the coal was a red piece of iron, forming a huge griddle more than half a yard across. The bread matched this very nearly in size when it was ready to be baked, and it was spread out and turned upon the griddle with great dexterity, and as soon as it was baked it was added to a great heap on the floor.

'The woman said she should continue to bake bread for thirty days. She had a large family of men who consumed a great deal, and they had to bake very often in consequence. In many places they do not bake bread oftener than twice a year, then it is a circumstance like haying or harvesting. We heard an Englishman say of this bread of the country: "One might eat an acre of it and then not be satisfied."'

In Denmark, too, rye bread is the rule among the

73

The History of Bread

peasantry and small farmers—wheaten bread being to them a luxury, and used as cake is with us. In Russia, although its chief export is wheat from the Black Sea, and oats and rye from the Baltic, the peasant eats but rye bread dipped in hemp oil, and even then, as but a few years since, famine visits this granary, and the hapless peasants being reduced to mix orach and bark with their wretched bread, have at times been unable to procure even this, and have died in thousands of starvation. Although Austria-Hungary produces wheat which makes the finest bread-flour in the world, yet throughout the Austrian Empire the peasantry eat rye bread, whilst at Vienna the wheaten bread, especially the *Kaiser semmel*, which is what we should term a dinner roll or manchet, is simply perfection.

The excellence of the Viennese bread is said to be owing to the bakers, the ovens, and the yeast. The men work according to the traditions of the past, which have been handed down to them. The ovens are heated by wood fires lit inside them during four hours ; the ashes are then raked out, and the oven is carefully wiped with wisps of damp straw. On the vapour thus generated, as well as that produced by the baking of the dough, lies the whole art of the browning and the success of the *semmel*. An ounce of yeast (three decagrammes) and as much salt is taken for every gallon of milk used for the dough. The yeast is a Viennese speciality, known as *St. Marxner Pressheffe*, and its composition is a secret. It keeps two days in summer and a little longer in winter.

Viennese bread is noted for the fantastic shapes

.into which it is made, but concerning the crescent shape the following legend is told : ' Many years ago, when there was war between the Austrians and the Turks, the city of Vienna was besieged, and so closely invested that famine seemed inevitable unless the inhabitants yielded and surrendered to the hated Turks. One day a baker in his cellar noticed a peculiar noise, and, looking about, discovered that a boy's drum on the ground in a corner had some marbles on the parchment, which every little while danced about and caused the odd sound. Surprised, he listened intently, and found that the noise was repeated at regular intervals. He put his ear to the ground and could distinguish a thumping sound, which, on reflection, he concluded must be produced by the enemy undermining the city. He went to the authorities with his story, but at first it was discredited. At last the general in command made an investigation, and found the baker's suspicions correct. A counter-mine was made and exploded, and the Turks repulsed.

On the restoration of peace, the Emperor of Austria sent for the baker, and expressing his gratitude to him for having saved the city, asked what reward he could claim. The modest baker refused riches or rank, but only asked the privilege of making his bread hereafter in the form of the crescent, which had so long been their terror, so that it might be a reminder to those who ate it that the God of the Christian is greater than the God of the Infidel. So the Imperial order was issued granting the baker and his descendants the sole right

The History of Bread

to make their bread in the shape of the Turkish crescent.'

As in Austria, so in Germany. Good wheaten bread can be got in towns and cities, though not so fine as in Austria, by reason of the flour, and the peasantry are content to have rye and barley bread. *Pumpernickel*, to wit, is one of the oldest varieties of bread, and the first to come into general use. It is made of barley, and must be baked in an oven especially made for the purpose. This kind of bread is considered very nutritious, and is of a sweet taste. In many parts of Germany there are large bakeries where *pumpernickel* is baked as a speciality, whence it is sent into the smaller towns, and even exported to other countries in loaves of 4 lbs., 8 lbs., and 12 lbs. weight. At Soest, Unna, and Brostadt large quantities are made for exportation, for the expatriated German carries his love of Fatherland with him, and at Berlin there is also a bakery for making *pumpernickel*.

The Gauls reaped their wheat, and then threshed it out by means of oxen and horses ; but they also cut off the ears, and then reaped the straw. To gather in the panic and millet, they held the stalks by means of a kind of comb, and then cut off the heads with shears. To prevent its being stolen, the corn was hidden in underground storehouses, and often in natural caves, which were afterwards walled up. They used mealing stones, as before described, in order to crush and roughly grind their grain, which was made into an unleavened cake, dry and thin, which was not cut, but was broken when served. They also had a kind of bread called ' plate bread,' which they ate soaked with sauce or meat gravy. The Gauls made beer from barley, and used it instead of water to mix their dough with. Thus, unconsciously, they discovered the secret of leavened bread; and, by-and-by, noticing that the beer if let alone frothed, and that when used for bread-making in this state the bread was lighter, they left off using the beer, and only employed the yeast.

Barley they called *gru*, which, in Latin, became *grudum*. *Gruellum* was husked barley, which the Gauls ate in soup and with boiled meat. This is the origin of the French word *gruau* (groats), which is equally applied to husked oats. Rye was used in the northern part of Gaul; and, from the time of Strabo, millet was in use among the Gauls as well as panic, but especially in Aquitaine. They also certainly knew of buck-wheat, which had been cultivated from time immemorial in Africa, for it has been found in several Celtic remains in the Camp de Chalons.

The Romans brought millstones with them, and introduced the water-wheel, which saved them the exertion of personally grinding their corn, and with the arrival of the Franks came Christianity, and they were taught the prayer, 'Our Father, which art in Heaven . . . . give us this day our daily bread.'

In the twelfth and thirteenth centuries in France, noblemen, the middle-class, and shopkeepers did not eat much white bread, and their best was equal to the 'household bread' of to-day, whilst whitey-brown, brown, and bran breads were to be found on their tables. The common folk fed on bread made of

The History of Bread

barley, rye, maslin, a mixture of wheat and rye, brown bread, black bread, and enormous pasties, of which the thick crust was composed of rye, bran, and flour mixed together.

Maize was introduced into France from America in 1560. Champier speaks of it as a plant recently imported, and says: 'Some poor people, in default of corn, have made bread of it, especially in the Beaujolais, but it is less fitted for men than for animals, which fatten quickly upon it, and especially for pigeons who love it much.'

Vermicelli, macaroni, lazagnes (riband vermicelli) and other Italian pastes were brought into France during the wars of Charles VIII., and had no other rivals than rice.

At this time, in making bread, the yeast of beer was partially abandoned, and other ferments were made use of. The Flemings boiled wheat, and, after having skimmed off the froth, used it as a leaven, which gave them a bread much lighter than hitherto, or, according to Champier and Liébaut, who wrote in 1589, they employed vinegar, wine, and rennet; and from their writings we find that the farmers were their own millers and bakers.

'It would be useless for the labourer to take so much pains with his land, if he only derived a profit from a sale of the grain which he has harvested, if he could not himself make cakes, flammèches (*flaky pastry*), flans (*cakes made with flour, eggs, milk and butter*), fritters, and a thousand other dainties, which he can make with a flour from his own corn; and it would be very unbecoming in him were he to borrow them from his neighbours, or buy them of the bakers or pastrycooks.

'The farmer's duty is to choose his corn, have it ground, and to keep the flour in the granary, whence he will soon take it in order to make bread. The

A MEDIÆVAL BAKERY.
(*From an engraving by Jost Amman*)

handling of the flour and kneading the dough is entirely the care of the wife, who ought to give all her best energies to it, for of all food bread is the best; one gets tired of the most delicate meats, but never of bread.'

From this time till the present there is no great

79

The History of Bread

story to tell of bread in France. It has progressed in quality, as in every other country, until French bread is famous throughout the civilised world. But this is mainly in the towns; black bread is still in use in some of the rural parts of France, and one can imagine the relish with which the peasant tastes once more the bread of his youth after having been deprived of it for some time.

In Paris, at one time, the monks controlled the bakery business; they had the monopoly of the public ovens, where housewives brought the dough to be baked, just as nowadays they take a shoulder of mutton and potatoes. But no baking was allowed on Sundays and fête days. France thus observed Sunday as a whole holiday, and the oven-tax went towards the support and burial of the poor. Up to 1789 the bakers were compelled to sell nearly all their bread at stalls in the public markets, and 900 master bakers monopolised the privilege; for it was only in 1863 that the trade became free and thrown open to all. Previous to that, in order to qualify for a master baker, it was necessary to graduate five years as an apprentice, and four more as a journeyman; also the sale of fancy bread was obliged to be carried on in an underhand way, and it was delivered in secret, being subject to a tax, and the baker not being able to make it of exact weight, without prejudice, on account of its great extent of crust.

American flour is celebrated all over the world, and is more extensively used in England, especially the finest sorts for pastry; but, of course, the demand for it in the immense continent itself is something

Bread in Europe and America

enormous. Take one instance, Philadelphia, which is celebrated for its good bread. Over one million barrels are sold in that city annually for home consumption, and two-thirds of this is made into bread. The 1300 bakers in Philadelphia use 600,000 barrels a barrel of good flour making from 270 to 280 five cent. loaves, and the best flour is the cheapest to use. As a rule, the bakers use choice brands, and mix four grades to get the proper alloy, so to speak—two 'Minnesota springs' and two 'Indiana winters.' Some bakers, especially those who make the best breads, use only one grade of spring wheat and two of winter. In the olden time yeast was made of malt, potatoes, and hops, and it is still largely used, but the bakers of fancy breads use a patent yellow compressed yeast. There are seven large steam bread bakeries in Philadelphia, giving employment to three or four hundred hands. One large establishment manufactures the different varieties of Vienna bread exclusively. It is made of the best flour, and milk instead of water is used to mix the flour. The baking is done in air-tight ovens, and the steam generated in baking settles back on the bread instead of escaping. This makes the outer crust thin and tender, and gives the bread a particularly rich taste and pleasant aroma.

With the addition of maize and buckwheat, the Americans use the same cereals for making bread as we do; but, of course, as is the case with every nation, there are specialities which do not travel abroad. Graham bread is our wholemeal bread, and should be made with the unbolted meal of wheat, and not only that, but the wheat of which it is made should be good plump grain, otherwise there would be a disproportionate quantity of bran.

Then there is Boston brown bread, for which the following is the formula : One quart Indian corn meal, one quart Graham, one quart rye flour, one quart white flour, one quart boiling water, one pint yeast, one small cup of molasses, two teaspoonfuls of salt, half-cup of burnt sugar colouring. For rye and Indian corn bread it is only necessary to change the above recipe by leaving out the Graham and white flour and doubling the proportions of Indian corn meal and rye in their place.

Of rolls there are very many varieties besides the ordinary French rolls. Many hotels have their speciality in this class of bread, and, consequently, we have Parker, Tremont, Revere, Brunswick, Clarendon, St. James, Windsor, &c., rolls, besides which there are twist and sandwich rolls.

CHAPTER VII.

Early English Bread.

WHEN the culture of grain in Britain really commenced we cannot possibly tell, but we know that the Phœnicians traded with this island in very early times for tin. All that we really know is from the fragments of writing left by Pytheas, who may, in one sense, be said to have been the discoverer of Britain. About 340 B.C. the Greek colony which the Greeks had planted at Massilia (Marseilles) wished to extend their trade, and, whether at their expense or his own, Pytheas, a learned man, a geographer and astronomer, set sail for parts unknown in the Western Ocean.

Diodorus Siculus, who lived just before the Christian era, must have taken his account of the Britons from Pytheas. In Book V., c. 2, he says: 'They dwell in mean cottages, covered for the most part with reeds and sticks. In reaping their corn, they cut the ears from off the stalk, and house them in repositories under ground ; thence they take and pluck out the grains of as many of the oldest of them as may serve them for the day, and, after they have bruised the corn, make it into bread.'

It is said, also, that about this time the Britons exported corn to Gaul and also up the Rhine. On Cæsar's arrival he found them an agricultural people, with abundance of wheat and barley ; and during the time of the Roman occupation they made great advances in agriculture. After their departure a hide

of land was 180 acres if it was cultivated on the
Roman three-field system, or 160 if on the English
plan of two-field course. In the former, one portion
was sown with winter wheat, a second with spring
wheat, whilst the third lay fallow. The English way
was to divide the hide, and in each half to sow
alternately spring and winter wheat, and the chief
crops raised were rye, oats, barley, wheat, beans and
peas. In social rank, the yeoman, or geneat (tenant
farmer), ranked next after the thegn and the priest,
whilst even the baker was an important member of
a thegn's household—the bread being made in round
flat cakes from wholemeal (for there is no mention of
bolting it), ground in a hand-mill or quern. Such
were doubtless the storied cakes which Alfred watched
for the neatherd's wife.

The peasants' bread was principally made of rye,
oats, and beans, the wheat being used by the 'gentry'
only—ordinary bread being made of barley; and,
connected with the latter, are derived our names of
Lord and Lady, the first from *Llaford*, originator of
bread, or bread-ward, the latter from *Llœfdige*, bread-
maid, or bread-maker. So, too, we owe our wedding
cake to the great loaf made by the bride to show her
inauguration into housewifery, which was partaken of
by the wedding guests.

The peasant baked his bread on iron plates or in
rude ovens, and ground his coarse meal in hand-mills;
but in later times water was made the principal motive
power for grinding corn, and about 5000 mills are
mentioned in Domesday Book; but they are not
particularised as to what power they were worked by.

Early English Bread

As a trade, the bakers of London rank from a very early date. They formed a brotherhood, or guild, in the reign of Henry II., about 1155. Stow says of them : 'The Company of White Bakers are of great antiquity, as appeareth by their Records, and divers other things of antiquity, extant in their Common Hall. They were a Company of this City in the first year of Edward II., and had a new Charter granted unto them in the first year of Henry VII., the which Charter was confirmed unto them by Henry VIII., Edward VI., Queen Mary, Queen Elizabeth, and King James I. Their Arms were anciently borne ; the crest and supporters were granted to them by Robert Cook, *Clarencieux*, the Letters Patent bearing date November 8 (32 Eliz.), 1590. The Cloud on the Chief thro' which the Hand holding the Scales Cometh, hath a Glory, omitted in the edition printed 1633 ; and on each side of the Hand are two Anchors, here also omitted ; as by the Visitation Book, *Anno* 1634, appears.'

Stow describes the Company of the Brown Bakers as 'A Society of long standing and continuance, prevailed to have their Incorporating granted the ninth day of June, in the 19th year of the Reign of our Sovereign Lord King James I.'

The Arms of both White and Brown Bakers are copied from Harl. MSS. 1464, 57e. (73), A.D. 1634— the Arms of these and other Companies being copied from the Herald's Visitation of that year, by Rd. Price, Armes-Painter.

Heraldically described, the Arms of the White Bakers are—Gules, three Garbs Or, a chief barry wavy of four, argent and azure, an arm issuing from clouds radiated of the second, the hand holding a pair of scales depending between the upper Garbs,

THE ARMS OF THE WHITE BAKERS.

also of the second. *Crest:* Two Arms embowed issuing out of clouds, proper, holding in the hands a chaplet of wheat, or. *Supporters:* Two Stags, proper, attired, or, each gorged with a chaplet of wheat, of the last.

The Arms of the Brown Bakers closely resemble

ARMS OF THE BROWN BAKERS.

those of their white brethren, but are not so dignified, as lacking supporters and motto: Vert, a chevron quarterly, or and gules, charged with a pair of

The History of Bread

balances, azure, holden by a hand out of a cloud, proper, between three garbs of beans, rye and wheat, or. On a chief barry of five, wavy, argent and azure, an Anchor couchant, or. *Crest:* An Arm quarterly of the second, the hand holding a bean sheaf, proper.

W. Carew Hazlitt, in his *Livery Companies of the City of London* (Lond. 1892) says: 'In the Elizabeth, as in the Henry VIII. Charter, the White Bakers had taken the initiative in drawing the makers of brown bread, whose business was far more limited and unimportant, into union with them on unequal terms, and the latter body dissented and renounced; whereupon the Queen was advised by the Lords of the Council to recall her patent. This proceeding seems, for a time, to have caused the matter to drop; but in 19 James I., June 6, 1622, the Brown Bakers succeeded in securing separate incorporation, with a common seal, a Master, three Wardens, and sixteen Assistants, as well as all other usual rights and powers. We hear nothing further of the matter till 1629, when the two bodies were still separate, the White Bakers being assessed for a levy by the City in that year at £25 16s., the other at £4 6s., a proof of the relative weight and resources of the disputants, which is confirmed by the proportions contributed by each to the Ulster scheme a few years prior, namely, £480 and £90. In 1654 the Brown Bakers had apparently relinquished their independent quarters at Founders' Hall, Lothbury, as if an union had been arranged; and in 2 James II. the charter was received with the usual restrictions in regard to the oaths of allegiance and supremacy, and conformity to the Church of

Early English Bread

England, but otherwise in such a form as to lead to the belief that it comprehended both sections of the trade.'

The Bakers' Company ranks very high after the twelve great City Companies, on account of its great antiquity. Its Hall, in Stow's time, was in 'Hart Lane, or Harp Lane, which likewise runneth (*from Tower Street*) into Thames Street. In this Hart Lane is the Bakers' Hall, some time the dwelling-house of John Chichley, Chamberlain of London.' And in Harp Lane it still is. According to Whitaker's Almanack for 1904 its livery numbers 152 and its total income is only £1900.

Much early legislation was passed regarding bakers and their calling, but, in spite of it all, some bakers did not amend their ways, and an amusing grievance was made by Fabyan as to their punishment. In his *Chronicles*, under date of 1268, and speaking of the harshness of Sir Hugh Bigod, justice, he says: 'In processe of tyme after, the sayde syr Hughe, wt. other, came to Guylde hall, and kepte his courte and plees there withoute all ordre of lawe, and contrarye to the lybertyes of the cytie, and there punysshed the bakers for lacke of syze, by the tumberell, where before tymes they were punysshed by the pyllery, and orderynge many thynges at his wyll, more than by any good ordre of lawe.' And Holinshed repeats the story.

Nor were their misdeeds confined to their trade, as we may learn from the Archives of the City of London. In fact, their evil deeds were so notorious that the King himself had to take cognizance of them.

89

The History of Bread

That the bakers wanted looking after is well evidenced by the following extracts from the City archives :

26 Edward I., A.D. 1298. 'Be it remembered that on Wednesday next after the Feast of St. Lawrence (August 10), in the 26th year of the reign of King Edward, Juliana, la Pestour of Neutone (*the baker of Newington*), brought a cart laden with six shillings' worth of bread into West Chepe ; of which bread, that which was light bread was wanting in weight, according to the assise of the halfpenny loaf, to the amount of 25 shillings in weight. [The shilling of silver being three-fifths of an ounce in weight, this deficiency would be 15 ounces.] And of the said six shillings' worth, three shillings' worth was brown bread ; which brown bread was of the right assise. It was, therefore, adjudged that the same should be delivered to the aforesaid Juliana, by Henry le Galeys, Mayor of London, Thomas Romeyn, and other Aldermen. And the other three shillings' worth, by award of the said Mayor and Aldermen, was ordered to be given to the prisoners in Newgate.'

3. Edward II., A.D. 1310. 'On the Monday next before the Feast of St. Hilary (13th January), in the third year of the reign of Edward, the son of King Edward, the bread of Sarra Foting, Christina Terrice, Godiyeva Foting, Matilda de Bolingtone, Christina Pricket, Isabella Sperling, Alice Pegges, Joanna de Cauntebrigge, and Isabella Pouvestre, bakeresses of Stratford [The bread of London, in these times, was extensively made in the villages of Bromley (*Bremble*), Middlesex, and Stratford-le-Bow. Stow

Early English Bread

says, 'And because I have here before spoken of the
bread carts coming from Stratford at the Bow, ye
shall understand that of old time the bakers of bread
at Stratford were allowed to bring daily (except the

AN EARLY BAKERY.

Sabbath and principal feasts) divers long carts laden
with bread, the same being two ounces in the penny
wheat loaf heavier than the penny wheat loaf baked
in the City, the same to be sold in Cheape, three or
four carts standing there, between Gatheron's Lane

and Fauster's Lane end, one cart on Cornhill, by the
Conduit, and one other in Grasse Street. And I have
read that in the fourth year of Edward II., Richard
Reffeham being Mayor, a baker named John, of
Stratforde, for making bread less than the assise, was,
with a fool's hood on his head and loaves of bread
about his neck, drawn on a hurdle through the streets
of the City. Moreover, in the 44th of Edward III.,
John Chichester being Mayor of London, I read in
the *Visions of Piers Plowman,* a book so called, as
followeth :

> At Londone I leve,
> Liketh wel my waires ;
> And louren whan thei lakken hem.
> It is noght long y passed,
> There was a careful commune,
> Whan no cart came to towne
> With breed fro Stratforde :
> Tho gennen beggaris wepe,
> And werkmen were agast a lite ;
> This wole be thought longe.
> In the date of oure Drighte,
> In a drye Aprill.
> A thousand and thre hundred
> Twies twenty and ten,
> My waires were gesene
> Whan Chichestre was Maire.']

was taken by Roger le Paumer, Sheriff of London,
and weighed before the Mayor and Aldermen ; and
it was found that the halfpenny loaf weighed less than
it ought by eight shillings. But, seeing that the
bread was cold, and ought not to have been weighed
in such state, by the custom of the City, it was
agreed that it should not be forfeited this time. But,

in order that such an offence as this might not pass
unpunished, it was awarded as to bread so taken
that three halfpenny loaves should always be sold for
a penny, but that the bakeresses aforesaid should this
time have such penny.'

5. Edward II., A.D. 1311. 'The bread taken from
William de Somersete, baker, on the Thursday next
before the Feast of St. Laurence (10th August) in the
fifth year of the reign of King Edward, was examined
and adjudged upon befor Richer de Refham, Mayor,
Thomas Romayn, John de Wengrave, and other
Aldermen; and, because it was found that such
bread was putrid, and altogether rotten, and made
of putrid wheat, so that persons by eating that bread
would be poisoned and choked, the Sheriff was
ordered to take him, and have him here on the
Friday next after the Feast of St. Laurence; then
to receive judgment for the same.'

In the 1 Ed. III. (1327) a curious fraud was
brought to light, and John Brid and seven other
bakers, and two bakeresses, were tried before the
Mayor and Aldermen, 'for that the said John, for
falsely and maliciously obtaining his own private
advantage, did skilfully and artfully cause a certain
hole to be made upon a table of his, called a *molding
borde* pertaining to his bakehouse, after the manner of
a mouse-trap, in which mice are caught, there being
a certain wicket warily provided for closing and
opening such hole.

'And when his neighbours and others, who were
wont to bake their bread at his oven, came with their
dough, or material for making bread, the said John

The History of Bread

used to put the said dough or other material upon the said table, called a *molding borde*, as aforesaid, and over the hole before mentioned, for the purpose of making loaves therefrom for baking ; and such dough or material being so placed upon the table aforesaid, the same John had one of his household, ready provided for the same, sitting in secret beneath such table ; which servant of his, so seated beneath the hole, and carefully opening it, piecemeal, and bit by bit, craftily withdrew some of the dough aforesaid, frequently collecting great quantities of such dough, falsely, wickedly, and maliciously, to the great loss of all his neighbours and persons living near, and of others who had come to him with such dough to bake, and to the scandal and disgrace of the whole City, and, in especial, of the Mayor and Bailiffs for the safe keeping of the assizes of the City assigned. Which hole, so found in his table, aforesaid, was made of aforethought ; and, in like manner, a great quantity of such dough that had been drawn through the said hole was found beneath the hole, and was, by William de Hertynge, serjeant-at-mace, and Thomas de Morle, clerk of Richard de Rothynge, one of the Sheriffs of the City aforesaid, who had found such material, or dough, in the suspected place before mentioned, upon oath brought here into Court.'

All the prisoners pleaded *Not Guilty ;* but the case was too clear against them, and ' It was agreed, and ordained, that all those of the bakers aforesaid, beneath whose tables with holes dough had been found, should be put upon the pillory, with a certain

Early English Bread

quantity of such dough hung from their necks; and that those bakers in whose houses dough was not found beneath the tables aforesaid, should be put upon the pillory, but without dough hung from their necks; and that they should so remain upon the pillory until Vespers at St. Paul's in London should be ended.' The women were committed to Newgate.

There was another punishment by which bakers, in common with all who told lies, or libelled, or scandalised their neighbour, had to stand in the pillory with a whetstone hung round their neck.

England suffered much from dearth. Holinshed tells us how, in 1149, 'The great raine that fell in the summer season did much hurt unto corne standng on the ground, so that a great dearth followed. 1175.—The same yeare both England and the countries adjoining were sore vexed with great mortalitie of people, and immediatlie after followed a sore dearth and famine. 1196.—Here is also to be noted, that in this seventh yeare of King Richard, chanced a dearth through this realme of England, and in the coasts about the same. 1199.—Furthermore I find that in the daies of this King Richard a great dearth reigned in England, and also in France, for the space of three or foure yeares during the wars betweene him and King Philip, so that, after his returne out of Germaine, and from imprisonment, a quarter of wheat was sold at eighteen shillings eight pence, no small price in those daies, if you consider the alay of monie then currant.

'1222.—Likewise on the day of the exaltation of the Crosse, a generall thunder happened through-

out the realme, and thereupon followed a continuall
season of foule weather and wet, till Candlemas next
after, which caused a dearth of corne, so as wheat was
sold at twelve shillings the quarter.

'1245.—Again the King, of purpose, had consumed all the provision of corne and vittels which
remained in the marshes, so that in Cheshire, and
other parts adjoining, there was such dearth that the
people scarse could get sufficient vittels to susteine
themselves withall.

'1258.—In this yeare was an exceeding great
dearth, insomuch that a quarter of wheat was sold
at London for foure and twentie shillings, whereas
within two or three yeares before, a quarter was sold
at two shillings. It had been more dearer, if great
store had not come out of Almaine; for in France
and in Normandie it also failed. But there came
fiftie great ships fraught with wheat and barlie, with
meale and bread out of Dutch land, by the procure-
ment of Richard, King of Almaine, which greatlie
releeved the poore; for proclamation was made, and
order taken by the King, that none of the citizens of
London should buy anie of that graine to laie it up
in store, whereby it might be sold at an higher price
unto the needie. But, though this provision did much
ease, yet the want was great over all the realme.
For it was certainlie affirmed that in three shires
within the realme there was not found so much graine
of that yeare's growth as came over in those fiftie
ships. The proclamation was set forth to restrein the
Londoners from ingrossing up that graine, and not
without cause; for the wealthie citizens were evill

spoken of in that season, bicause in time of scarcitie they would either staie such ships as, fraught with vittels, were comming towards the citie, and send them some other way forth, or else buy the whole, that they might sell it by retaile, at their pleasure, to the needie. By means of this great dearth and scarcitie, the common people were constrained to live upon herbs and roots, and a great number of the poore people died through famine. They died so thicke that there were great pits made in churchyards to laie the dead bodies in, one upon another.

'1289.—There insued such continuall raine, so distempering the ground, that corne waxed verie deare, so that whereas wheat was sold before at three pence a bushell, the market so rose by little and little that it was sold for two shillings a bushell, and so the dearth increased still almost for the space of 40 yeares, till the death of Edward the Second, in so much that sometimes a bushel of wheat, London measure, was sold at ten shillings. 1294.—This yeare in England was a great dearth and scarcity of corne, so that a quarter of wheat in manie places was sold for thirtie shillings ; by reason whereof poor people died in manie places for lack of sustnance.

'1316.—The dearth, by reason of the unseason-able weather in the summer and harvest last past, still increased, for that which with much ado was inned, after, when it came to the proofe, yeelded nothing to the value of that which in sheafe it seemed to conteine, so that wheat and other graine which was at a sore price before, now was inhanced to a farre

The History of Bread

higher rate, the scarcitie thereof being so great that a quarter of wheat was sold for fortie shillings, which was a great price, if we shall consider the allaie of monie then currant. Also, by reason of the murren that fell among cattell, beefes and muttons were unreasonablie priced. . . . . . In this season vittles were so scant and deere, and wheat and other graine brought to so high a price, that the poore people were constreined through famine to eat the flesh of horses, dogs, and other vile beasts, which is wonderfull to beleeve, and yet, for default, there died a great multitude of people in divers places of the land. Foure pence in bread of the coarser sort would not suffice one man a daie. Wheat was sold at London for foure marks a quarter and above. Then after this dearth and scarcitie of vittels issued a great death and mortalitie of people ; so that what by warres of the Scots, and what by this mortalitie and death, the people of the land were wonderfullie wasted and consumed. O pitifull depopulation !

'1335.—This yeare there fell great abundance of raine, and thereupon insued morren of beasts ; also corne so failed this yeare that a quarter of wheat was sold at fortie shillings. 1353.—In the summer of this season and twentieth yeare, was so great a drought, that from the latter end of March fell little raine till the latter end of Julie, by reason whereof manie inconveniences insued ; and one thing is specially to be noted, that corne the yeare following waxed scant, and the price began this yeare to be greatlie inhanced. Also beeves and muttons waxed deare for the want of grasse ; and this chanced both in England and

Early English Bread

France, so that this was called the deere summer. The Lord William, Duke of Baviere or Bavaria, and Earl of Zelund brought manie ships in London fraught with rie for the releefe of the people, who otherwise had, through their present pinching penurie, if not utterlie perished yet pittifullie pined.

' 1370.—By reason of the great wet and raine that fell this yeare in more abundance than had been accustomed much corne was lost, so that the price thereof was sore inhanced, in so much that wheat was sold at three shillings four pence the bushell. 1389.—Herewith followed a great dearth of corne, so that a bushell of wheat in some places was sold at thirteen pence, which was thought to be a great price. 1394.—In this yeare was a great dearth in all parts of England, and this dearth or scarcitie of corne began under the sickle, and lasted till the feast of Saint Peter *ad Vincula*—to wit, till the time of new corne. This scarcitie did greatly oppresse the people, and chieflie the commoners of the poorer sort. For a man might see infants and children in streets and houses, through hunger, howling, crieing, and craving bread, whose mothers had it not (God wot) to breake unto them. But yet there was such plentie and abundance of manie years before, that it was thought and spoken of manie housekeepers and husbandmen, that if the seed were not sowen in the ground, which was hoorded up and stored in barnes, lofts, and garners, there would be enough to find and susteine all the people by the space of five years following. . . . The scarcity of victuals was of greatest force in Leicestershire, and in the middle parts of

The History of Bread

the realme. And although it was a great want, yet was not the price of corne out of reason. For a quarter of wheat, when it was at the highest, was sold at Leicester for 16 shillings 8 pence at one time, and at other times for a market of 14 shillings; at London and other places of the land a quarter of wheat was sold for 10 shillings, or for little more or lesse. For there arrived eleven ships laden with great plentie of victuals at diverse places of the land, for the reliefe of the people. Besides this, the citizens of London laid out two thousand marks to buy food out of the common chest of orphans, and the foure and twentie aldermen, everie of them put in his twentie pounds apeece for necessarie provision, for feare of famine likelie to fall upon the cities. And they laid up their store in sundrie of the fittest and most convenient places they could choose, that the needie and such as were wrong with want might come and buy at a certaine price so much as might suffice them and their families ; and they which had not readie monie to paie downe presentlie in hand, their word and credit was taken for a yeare's space next following, and their turn served. Thus was provision made that people should be relieved, and that none might perish for hunger.

' 1439.—This yeare (by reason of great tempests, raging winds, and raine) there arose such scarsitie that wheat was sold at three shillings foure pence the bushell. . . . Whereupon Steven Browne, at the same season maior of London, tendering the state of the Citie in this want of bread corne, sent into Pruse certeine ships, which returned laden with

Early English Bread

plentie of rie ; wherewith he did much good to the people in that hard time, speciallie to them of the Citie, where the want of corne was not so extreame as in some other places of the land, where the poore distressed people that were hunger-bitten made them bred of ferne roots, and used other hard shifts, till God provided remedie for their penurie by good successe of husbandrie. 1527.—By reason of the great wet that fell in the sowing time of the corne, and in the beginning of the last yeare ; now, in the beginning of this, corne so failed, that in the Citie of London, for a while, bread was scant, by reason that the commissioners appointed to see order taken in shires about, ordcined that none should be conveied out of one shire into another. Which order had like to have bred disorder, for that everie countrie and place was not provided alike, and namelie London, that maketh her provision out of other places, felt great inconvenience thereby, till the merchants of the Stillard and others out of the Dutch countries brought such plentie that it was better cheape in London than in anie other part of England, for the King also releeved the citizens in time of their need with a thousand quarters, by waie of lone, of his owne provision.'

By the foregoing we see that the bad dearths came at longer intervals, probably owing to better husbandry, and the regular importation of foreign corn before a scarcity could arise. But, on the other side, I have to chronicle a few (unfortunately only too few) years of exceeding plenty. The first one recorded was in 1288, and is thus recorded by Stow: 'The

The History of Bread

summer was so exceeding hote this yeere that many men died through heate, and yet wheate was solde at London for three shillings foure pence the quarter when it was dearest, and in other partes abroad the same was sold for twentie pence or sixteen pence the quarter; yea, for twelve pence the quarter, and in the west and north parts for eight pence the quarter; barley for six pence, and oats for foure pence the quarter, and such cheapnesse of beanes and pease as the like had not been heard. 1317.—This yeere was an early harvest, so that all the corne was inned before St. Giles day (Sep. 1). A bushel of wheat that was before for X shillings was solde for ten pence; and a bushel of otes that before was eyght. shillings was solde for eyght pence.'

Holinshed tells us that in 1493 wheat was sold in London at 6d. the bushel; and in 1557.—'This yeare, before harvest wheat was sold for foure marks the quarter, malt at foure and fortie shillings the quarter, and pease at six and fortie shillings and eight pence; but, after harvest, wheat was sold for five shillings the quarter, malt at six shillings eight pence, rie at three shillings foure pence. So that the penie wheat loafe that weied in London the last yeere but eleven ounces Troie weied now six and fiftie ounces Troie. In the countrie wheat was sold for foure shillings the quarter, malt at foure shillings eight pence; and, in some places a bushell of rie for a pound of candles, which were foure pence.'

CHAPTER VIII.

HOW GRAIN BECOMES FLOUR.

IN order to make bread, the first operation is to grind the corn, be it wheat, rye, barley, or oats, and we have already seen the rough methods used by primitive man and others to effect this; we have noted the mealing stones, the pestle and mortar, the hand quern, and the grinding of corn by the Greeks and Romans. They soon gave up man as a motive power, and substituted mules or horses; these in their time gave place to water, which is a cheap and, if there be anything like a fall, a very powerful motor—hence the mills dotted all over the country, by the side of brook or river, with their water-wheels either over or undershot. Very picturesque are they mostly, and the drowsy murmur of the wheel and the gentle splashing of the water are very pleasant. We are seeing the last of them; they have done their work and must be thrown aside, for no one in his senses, who had water-power, would now erect water-wheels when he could get a turbine.

As with the water-wheel, so its congener, the windmill, beloved of artists, is going. A motive power as cheap as water is the wind, but, unfortunately, it is not so reliable. It is believed that the Chinese were the first to use the wind as a motive power for mills, and we have no record as to when they were introduced into Europe; we only know they were in use in the twelfth century. As a rule, in England, windmills have four arms, or 'whips,' but sometimes they have six. These arms are generally covered with strong canvas, but occasionally they are covered with thin boarding; they are set at an angle, which

A POST MILL.

varies according to the fancy of the miller, but the shaft to which they are attached (called the 'wind shaft') is invariably placed at an inclination of 10 or 15 degrees, in order that the revolving arms should clear the bottom portion of the mill.

The oldest kind of windmill is called a *post* mill,

A WATER-WHEEL MILL.

105

The History of Bread

because the whole structure is centred on a post, or pivot, and, when the wind shifts, the mill has to be turned bodily to meet it, by means of a long lever. The *smock*, or *frock*, windmill is an improvement upon the post mill; the building itself is stationary and permanent, but the head or cap, where is the wind shaft, rotates, and this is more easily managed.

For hundreds of years people were contented with the four and six arms to their windmills, and it was only in modern times that Messrs. J. Warner and Sons, of Cripplegate, London, patented their annular sails, which, as is plain to the meanest capacity, are vastly superior. The shutters, or 'vanes,' are connected with spiral springs, which keep them up to the best angle of weather for light winds. If the strength of the wind increases, the vanes give to the wind, forcing back the springs, and thus the area on which the wind acts diminishes. In addition, there are a striking lever and tackle for setting the vanes edgeways to the wind, when the mill is stopped, or a storm expected.

We have seen how from the very first man used stones wherewith to triturate his corn, and to this day stones are still used for grinding, although their days are in all probability numbered, and in a very little time they, with the windmill, will be relegated to limbo. The *Encyclopædia Britannica* gives such an excellent description of these mill-stones, that I quote it in its entirety.

'They consist of two flat cylindrical masses inclosed within a wooden or sheet metal case, the lower, or *bed-stone*, being permanently fixed, while the upper, or *runner*, is accurately pivoted and balanced over it. The average size of millstones is about four feet two inches in diameter, by twelve inches in thickness, and they are made of a hard but cellular siliceous stone, called buhr-stone, the best qualities of which are obtained from La-Ferté-sous-Jouarre, department of Seine et Marne, France. Millstones are generally

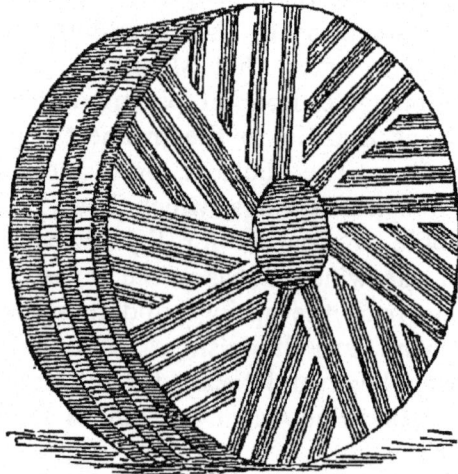

The Grinding Surface of a Millstone.

built up of segments, bound together round the circumference by an iron hoop, and backed with plaster of Paris. The bed-stone is dressed to a perfectly flat plane surface, and a series of grooves, or shallow depressions, are cut in it, generally in the manner shown, which represents the grinding surface of an upper or running stone. The grooves on both are made to correspond exactly, so that when the one is rotated over the other the sharp edges of the grooves meeting each other, operate like a rough pair of scissors, and thus the effect of the stones on grain submitted to their action is at once that of cutting, squeezing, and crushing. The dressing and grooving of millstones is generally done by hand picking, but sometimes black amorphous diamonds (*carbonado*) are used, and emery wheel dressers have likewise been suggested. The upper stone, or runner, is set in motion by a spindle on which it is mounted, which passes up through the centre of the bed-stone, and there are screws and other appliances for adjusting and balancing the stone. Further provision is made within the stone case for passing through air to prevent too high a heat being developed in the grinding operation, and sweepers for conveying the flour to the meal spout are also provided.

'The ground meal delivered by the spout is carried forward in a conveyor, or creeper box, by means of an Archimedean screw, to the elevators, by which it is lifted to an upper floor to the bolting or flour-dressing machine. The form in which this apparatus was formerly employed consisted of a cylinder mounted on an inclined plane, and covered externally with wire cloth of different degrees of fineness, the finest being at the upper part of the cylinder, where the meal is admitted. Within the cylinder, which was stationary, a circular brush revolved, by which the meal was pressed against the wire cloth, and, at the same time, carried gradually towards the lower extremity, sifting out, as it proceeded, the mill products into different grades of fineness, and finally delivering the coarse bran at the extremity of the

How Grain Becomes Flour

cylinder. For the operation of bolting or dressing, hexagonal or octagonal cylinders, about three feet in diameter, and from 20 to 25 feet long, are now commonly employed. These are mounted horizontally on a spindle for revolving, and externally they are covered with silk of different degrees of fineness, whence they are called "silks," or "silk dressers." Radiating arms or other devices for carrying the meal gradually forward as the apparatus revolved, are fixed within the cylinders; and there is also an arrangement of beaters, which gives the segments of cloth a sharp tap, and thereby facilitates the sifting action of the apparatus. Like all other mill machines, the modifications of the silk dresser are numerous.'

We have seen the ordinary operation of grinding flour in the old-fashioned way; now let us notice the improvements in making wheat into flour.

'We will suppose that the wheat has arrived by lighter at one of the large mills on the Thames, and that it has been shovelled into sacks and hoisted into the warehouse. The process by which it is turned into flour may be divided into three stages: (1) cleaning, (2) breaking, (3) grinding; but the number and complexity of the operations included in these stages are astounding. It must be understood that the following description refers to a first-class London mill—that is, one which has, certainly no superior, and, probably, no equal, in the world.

'In the first stage the wheat is merely prepared for the mill, and this is done in the cleaning department, which is separate from the mill proper. From the warehouse the grain is passed to a sifter or "separator,"

The History of Bread

which is a kind of sieve. Here the grosser impurities—straw, sticks, stones, earth, seeds, and what not—are removed. Thence to an "elevator," precisely similar in principle to that previously described, and by the elevator straight to the top of the building. Here it enters a wire sieve in the form of a revolving hexagonal "reel," by which the smaller heavy impurities with which it is still mixed are separated. Passing through this, it drops into the next storey, to be subjected to the "aspirator," an apparatus by means of which currents of air are blown through the grain as it falls and carry off the lighter and more volatile rubbish mixed with it. In the next floor is an ingenious instrument with a special purpose. Among the wheat is still a quantity of small black seeds, known as "cockle" seeds, and to get rid of these the "cockle cylinder" is employed. It is a revolving metal cylinder, the inner surface of which is fitted with small holes ; the grain passes into the interior of the cylinder, and as the latter goes round and round the cockle seeds stick in the small holes and are carried up to a certain height, when they fall out and are caught by an "apron" ; while the wheat, which is too large to stick in the holes, continually falls back into the bottom of the cylinder. Again our corn drops a storey, and encounters the "decorcitator." The object of this apparatus is to knock off the dust and dirt adhering to the grains, and it is effected by agitating them between two metal surfaces at a high rate of speed. The amount of dust removed by this method from apparently clean grain is astonishing. In the next storey is another decorcitator, and below that

How Grain Becomes Flour

a second aspirator, which brings us once more to the ground.

'On reaching the ground floor again, our now clean wheat is first passed through the "grading" or "sizing" reels, which separate it into two sizes, and then it enters the mill proper. It should be said here that the milling industry of the world has been revolutionised within the past few years by the substitution of steel rollers for the old millstones. The process of crushing or grinding, however, by steel rollers is accomplished in a very gradual manner, as will be explained: First come the "break rolls." These are solid steel rollers set in pairs, with corrugated surfaces; this gives them a cutting action. Wheat is passed through five successive pairs of these rollers. The first are about $\frac{1}{16}$th inch apart, and only break or bruise the grain slightly. Each successive pair is set closer, and carries the bruising a step further. But this is only half the business. After each set of rollers the grain goes through a "purifier," which is either a sieve of some kind or an aspirator, or both together, and the object is always the same—namely, to separate the solid particles of the broken wheat from the lighter ones. The former are, or rather will eventually be, flour; the latter constitute "offal." And the whole art of milling is merely an extension of this process; first reduction, then separation, repeated over and over again. As the grain passes through each successive set of rollers it is broken up finer and ever finer, and the separating action of the "purifier" accompanies it step by step. The solid particles grow smaller and smaller, the

111

The History of Bread

"offal" correspondingly finer and finer. This is the process in brief, but there are endless complications and refinements on the way. For instance, the solid particles are not only separated but are themselves divided into groups according to size. Then the offal often undergoes a further purifying process. Then the purifiers differ—some are complex, others simple; some of wire, others of silk; some revolve, others oscillate; some are "aspirated," others not; and so forth. Meanwhile, at the end of the five rolls and five purifiers, which make up our breaking department, we have got three products: (*a*) semolina; (*b*) middlings; (*c*) offal. The first two are practically varieties of the same—*i.e.*, both solid particles, which will afterwards be flour, but of different sizes. They are half way between grain and flour — hence the term "middlings."

'Grinding is only a continuation of the above process, but the rollers are different; their surfaces are smooth, and they are set closer together. The purifiers, too, are, for the most part, more elaborate. A look at one of them will show the extreme ingenuity expended on these operations. It consists primarily of an oscillating sieve made of silk, through the meshes of which the particles of flour fall into a wooden bin. On the floor of the bin is a "worm" which continually works the flour along to one end; on the under surface of the sieve is a travelling brush which brushes off the adhering flour and prevents the meshes from getting clogged. Above the sieve is an apparatus which, with the aid of currents blown by an aspirator, catches the volatile offal; and above that again a travelling blanket which arrests the still more volatile particles. Finally, the blanket, as it reaches the end, is tapped automatically to knock out what has stuck to it. By the time a handful of grain has been converted into a handful of fine flour it has gone through some 50 different machines, including 18 sets of rollers and 18 purifiers.

'The following points may be of interest: A first-class London mill working 100 sets of rollers can turn out 45 sacks of flour per hour. Offal, according to its fineness or coarseness, forms bran, pollard, etc, and is worth from 5*l.* to 6*l.* a ton. The qualities of flour are whiteness and strength. The former is tested by the eye, the latter only really by baking capacity. There seems to be a general consensus of opinion in favour of flour made from Hungarian wheat. The best English is of sweeter flavour, but lacks "strength." It has been reckoned that 300 sacks are made per hour in London mills, all of which is consumed in London. The flour mill industry owes nothing to American inventive genius; on the contrary, that country is behind the times. The steel rollers came originally from Hungary—always a great milling country.'

CHAPTER IX.

THE MILLER AND HIS TOLLS.

IN old times corn mills were always important factors in manors, and a source of considerable profit to the lord of the same. All the tenants of the manor were bound by custom to have their corn ground at the manor mill, paying a toll to the lord, for the mill was part of his demesne. The tenants owed suit to the mill in the same manner as they owed suit and service at the Manor Court. This, however, did not apply to the grinding or bruising of malt, and there were probably two good reasons for it — one, that the tenants could perform the operation on their own premises ; and the second, that if it were done at the mill it would be likely to spoil the flour next ground.

Very many instances of these mills may be given, but one will suffice, more especially as in this case it was carried down to modern times. There was at Wakefield, Yorkshire, a corn mill which was a franchise of the Pilkington family, of Chevel Park, by charters from one of the Edwards. The monopoly of grinding the corn at this mill was a great sore to the inhabitants, and the cause of much litigation, but the holders of the rights always came off the victors. They claimed the right of grinding not only for the town of Wakefied, but for some miles round, including the villages of Horbury, Ossett, Newmillardam, and others ; so that

The Miller and His Tolls

all the corn used in this district was obliged to be ground at the 'Soke Mill,' or, as it was otherwise called, the 'King's Mill,' and neither meal nor flour could be sold unless it were ground there. The tenant of the mill demanded a 'mulcture' of one-sixteenth—that is, out of 16 sacks of corn he kept one for himself for grinding the other 15.

Some time about 1850 the inhabitants of Wakefield and the adjacent villages determined to purchase the rights, and this was done by a rate spread over a series of years, and called the 'Soke Rate.' The purchase money amounted to about £20,000. The same kind of property existed at Leeds and at Bradford; but from neglect on the part of the owners, and lapse of time, the inhabitants turned restive and independent, and 'broke the Soke,' without compensating the Lords of the Manors. These mills are still called the King's Mills.

Nor was this custom confined to England. In Scotland, in feudal times, it was common for the tenants of a barony to be bound to have their corn ground at the barony mill. Centuries ago the erection of a substantial building, with the millstones, driving machinery, and other plant necessary for a mill, together with the drying-kilns, mill-dams, lades, weirs, and watercourses requisite for a corn mill involved the expenditure of a considerable sum of money, such as only the baron could find. He, therefore, assured himself of a return for his capital invested by binding his tenants to use his mill. Of course, he got a good rent for his mill, which was the manner in which the benefit arising

The History of Bread

from the bondage of his tenants found its way into his coffers.

Sir James A. Picton, in his *City of Liverpool* selections from the municipal archives and records, states that in 1558 the Corporation of the Borough ordered that 'every miller, on warning, shall bring his toll-dish to Mr. Mayor, to a lawful size thereof sealed, under a penalty of 6d.' That this toll-taking on the part of millers was occasionally perverted there can be but little doubt, and it was sometimes very severely commented on, as we may see in this passage from a tragedy by Wm. Sampson (1636), called *The Vow-Breaker ; or, the Fair Maid of Clifton*. 'Fellow Bateman, farewell ; commend me to my old windmill at Rudington. Oh ! the mooter dish—[Multure or Toll-dish]—the miller's thumbe, and the maide behind the hopper !'

In the Roxburghe ballads (vol. iii., 681) we have *The Miller's Advice to his Three Sons in Taking of Toll*:

'There was a miller who had three sons,
And knowing his life was almost run,
He called them all, and asked their will,
If that to them he left his mill.

He called first for his eldest son,
Saying, "My life is almost run,
If I to you this mill do make,
What toll do you intend to take?"

"Father," said he, "my name is Jack.
Out of a bushel I'll take a peck,
From every bushel that I grind,
That I may a good living find."

The Miller and His Tolls

"Thou art a fool," the old man said.
"Thou hast not well learned thy trade.
This mill to thee I ne'er will give,
For by such toll no man can live."

He called for his middlemost son,
Saying, "My life is almost run.
If I to thee the mill do make,
What toll do you intend to take?"

"Father," says he, "my name is Ralph.
Out of a bushel I'll take it half,
From every bushel that I grind,
So that I may a good living find."

"Thou art a fool," the old man said;
"Thou hast not learned well thy trade.
This mill to you I ne'er can give,
For by such toll no man can live."

He called for his youngest son,
Saying, "My life is almost run.
If I to you this mill do make,
What toll do you intend to take?"

"Father," said he, "I am your only boy,
For taking toll is all my joy.
Before I will a good living lack,
I'll take it all, and forswear the sack."

"Thou art my boy," the old man said,
"For thou has well learned thy trade.
This mill to thee I'll give," he cried,
And then he clos'd his eyes, and died.'

To show the popular idea of a miller's integrity, I
may mention that the children in Somersetshire,
when they have caught a certain kind of large white
moth, which they call a *Miller*, chant over it this
refrain :

'Millery! millery! Dousty Poll!
How many sacks of corn hast thou stole?'

The History of Bread

and then they put the poor insect to death on account of its imaginary misdeeds.

Even Chaucer must have his gird at the miller :

'The millere was a stout carl for the nones,
Ful byg he was of brawn and eek of bones ;
That proved wel, for over al ther he cam
At wrastlygne he wolde have alwey the ram (¹).
He was short sholdred, brood, a thikke knarre (²),
There was no dore that he ne wolde heve of harre (³).
Or breke it at a reunying with his head
His berd, or any sowe or fox was reed,
And ther to brood, as though it were a spade
Upon the cope right of his nose he hade
A werte, and ther on stood a toft of herys,
Reed as the brustles of a sowes erys ;
His nose thirles (⁴) blake were and wyde ;
A swerd and a bokeler bar he by his syde ;
His mouth as greet was as a greet forneys,
He was a janglere and a goliardeys (⁵),
And that was moost of synne and harlotries,
Wel konde he stelen corne and totten thries (⁶),
And yet he hadde 'a thombe of gold' *pardee*
A whit cote and a blew hood wered he,
A bagge pipe wel konde he blowe and sowne,
And ther with al he broghte us out of towne.'

The 'thombe of gold' has somewhat puzzled commentators on Chaucer. One thing is certain : that a miller has been traditionally credited with a broad thumb, and the little fish the *Bullhead* is called *The Millers' Thumb*, from a fancied resemblance. Every one connected with the navy knows what the 'purser's thumb' is, from the legend that, when serving out their

¹ Prize.   ² Knot.   ³ Hinges.
⁴ Nostrils.   ⁵ Jongleur and joker.   ⁶ Took toll thrice.

118

The Miller and His Tolls

tots of rum to the men, his thumb was invariably inside the measure (doubtless necessitated by the rolling of the old men-of-war), which resulted in a large profit to himself during a long cruise, and this seems to illustrate Chaucer's meaning, especially as it occurs immediately after the miller's ill-gotten gains, that by putting his broad thumb into every measure he made thereby gold during the year.

But there is another and a kindlier explanation of the term, which rests on the authority of Constable, the painter, according to Yarrell, in his *History of British Fishes*, when writing of the Bullhead. 'The head of the fish is smooth, broad, and rounded, and is said to resemble exactly the form of a miller's thumb, as produced by a peculiar and constant action of the muscles in the exercise of a particular and most important part of his occupation. It is well known that all the science and tact of a miller are directed so to regulate the machinery of his mill that the meal produced shall be of the most valuable description that the operation of grinding will permit, when performed under the most advantageous circumstances. His profit or his loss, even his fortune or his ruin, depend upon the exact adjustment of all the various parts of the machinery in operation. The miller's ear is constantly directed to the note made by the running-stone in its circular course over the bed-stone, the exact parallelism of their two surfaces, indicated by a particular sound, being a matter of the first consequence ; and his hand is as constantly placed under the meal spout to ascertain, by actual contact, the character and qualities of the meal produced. The thumb, by a particular movement, spreads the sample over the fingers ; the thumb is the gauge of the value of the produce, and hence have arisen the saying of *worth a miller's thumb*, and *an honest miller hath a golden thumb*, in reference to the amount of profit that is the reward of his skill.'

Any notice of flour would, of course, be valueless without an analysis of its constituent parts, which, as anyone can understand, will vary in different wheats ; there can be no standard, because of the difference of the soils on which it grows, a fact which is fully borne out by the following tables by famous analysts. Jago (*The Chemistry of Wheat, Flour, and Bread, &c.* Brighton, 1886), quoting Bell, says :—

Constituents.	Wheat. Winter.	Wheat. Spring.	Long-eared Barley.	English Oats.	Maize.	Rye.	Caroline rice without husk.
Fat	1·48	1·56	1·03	5·14	3·58	1·43	0·19
Starch	63·71	65·86	63·51	49·78	64·66	61·87	77·66
Cellulose ...	3·03	2·93	7·28	13·53	1·86	3·23	Tr'ces
Sugar (as Cane) ...	2·57	2·24	1·34	2·36	1·94	4·30	0·38
Albumin, &c. insoluble in Alcohol	10·70	7·19	8·18	10·62	9·67	9·78	7·94
Other nitrogeneous matter soluble in Alcohol ...	4·83	4·40	3·28	4·05	4·60	5·09	1·40
Mineral matter	1·60	1·74	2·32	2·66	1·35	1·85	0·28
Moisture ...	12·08	14·08	13·06	11·86	12·34	12·45	12·15
Total ...	100·00	100·00	100·00	100·00	100·00	100·00	100·00

The Miller and His Tolls

Professor Graham, in a lecture delivered at the International Health Exhibition, London, July 3, 1884, quoting Lawes and Gilbert, says :—

Constituents.	Old Wheat.	Barley.	Oats.	Rye.	Maize	Rice.
Water	11·1	12·0	14·2	14·3	11·5	10·8
Starch	62·3	52·7	66·1	54·9	54·8	78·8
Fat	1·2	2·6	4·6	2·0	4·7	0·1
Cellulose	8·3	11·5	1·0	6·4	14·9	0·2
Gum and Sugar ...	3·8	4·2	5·7	11·3	2·9	1·6
Albuminoids ...	10·9	13·2	16·0	8·8	8·9	7·2
Ash	1·6	2·8	2·2	1·8	1·6	0·9
Loss, &c.	0·8	1·0	0·2	0·5	7·0	0·4
Total	100·0	100·0	100·0	100·0	100·0	100·0

Messrs. Wanklyn and Cooper (*Bread Analysis, &c.*, London, 1881) say that, according to their analysis, this wheaten flour, which is the flour commonly to be bought in this country, has the following composition :—

Water	16·5
Ash	0·7
Fat	1·5
Gluten	12·0
Vegetable Albumen	1·0
Modified Starch	3·5
Starch Granules	64·8
	100·0

A comparison of these tables by well-known analysts shows us, if we only take the single article of wheat, how the grain varies. Let me now say something about the constituents of wheat in as simple a form as possible.

The fat is of a yellow colour, and, as far as is known, is not a particularly valuable component part; but as all fats are foods, of course, it is of service.

The starch in wheat is the ordinary starch (of the best kind) of commerce; and, seeing that it forms the greater part of all breadstuffs, it naturally is an important element in them. In good, sound wheat the starch granules are whole; in sprouted wheat, or that heated by damp, they are rotted, and, consequently, the starch they contain is changed, more or less, into dextrin and sugar, and, consequently, a difference is made in the food value of the wheat.

Dextrin and sugar are small components of good wheat. The dextrin, no doubt, has a beneficial effect in small quantities, but not in large. Sugar, such as is found in wheat, affords the necessary amount of saccharine matter for fermentation.

Cellulose is more useful to the plant than to the miller, to whom it is as so much bran.

There are two kinds of albuminoids, or gluten, present in wheat—one insoluble, the other soluble in alcohol. The former makes what is called a 'strong bread,' and the latter acts, in bread-making, on the former, and, under the influence of yeast, it attacks the starch, converting it into dextrin and maltose.

The ash of wheat contains principally phosphoric acid and potassium; magnesium ranks next; then lime, silica, phosphate of iron, soda, chlorine, and sulphuric and carbonic acids.

CHAPTER X.

BREAD MAKING AND BAKING.

THE ordinary method of bread-making in London is as follows: The first process, when the bread is made with thick yeast, being to prepare a mixture of potatoes, yeast, and flour, by which the process of fermentation is to be produced in the dough.

Mr. George W. Austin, in his pamphlet on *Bread, Baking, and Bakers,*' says about the ferment: 'For each sack of flour (280 lbs.) about 8 lbs. or 10 lbs. of dry, mealy potatoes are taken, well boiled and mashed and washed through a strainer to take away the skin ; to this is added 12 or 14 quarts of water, at a temperature varying from 80 deg. to 90 deg., and a quart of thick brewers' yeast, or 1 lb. of compressed yeast—which is equal. Having well dissolved the yeast, and added 2 lbs. of flour, the mass is allowed to stand some three or four hours, until the head falls in through the escape of gas.' The next process is the preparation of the sponge. The trough and flour being ready, the ferment is taken, and, with the addition of 28 quarts of clear water, at á temperature of 80 deg. to 90 deg., is passed into the trough through a sieve or strainer, and the mass, being kept well together, is made up into a nice dry sponge. It is allowed to remain thus and ferment for another five or six hours, when it will have risen and formed a head, which is allowed to break. As soon as this head is broken it commences to rise again, and as soon as it has broken the second time the remainder of the flour is added, and the dough made as follows:

Two and a half pounds of salt dissolved in 28 quarts of clear water, at a temperature of 80 deg., and mixed well into what is termed 'the sponge,' with the remainder of the flour, the whole being broken up and well and thoroughly mixed and kneaded until the dough is uniform in material and consistency. It is then left to rise for another hour or more, when the dough is weighed out in pieces of the requisite size and speedily manipulated into the required shape. As the loaves are moulded they are placed on trays, covered with a light cloth (to prevent the dry and colder air forming a dry crust on the surface), and left to dry sufficiently before being placed in the oven. Before this is done the loaves are slightly brushed over with a small quantity of milk and water to improve the appearance of the outside of the loaf when it comes from the oven.

The oven is, for the purpose of baking bread, brought up to a heat of 400 deg. Fahr., and the bread, although seemingly baked by dry heat, is in reality boiled in the steam of the water which the bread contains.[1]

[1] Some careful investigations have been made by M. Balland on the temperature which is reached in the interior of a loaf of bread during baking, and the results are published in the *Comptes Rendus*, Paris. Delicate thermometers were inserted in the dough before placing it in the oven, and on the removal of the loaf the temperature recorded was carefully noted. It seems that, contrary to the opinions expressed by some investigators—that the heat generated in the crumb of the bread never exceeds 212° Fahr.—that is to say, the temperature of boiling water—M. Balland finds that it invariably attains from 212° to 216° Fahr., while that of the outer crust, which cannot form at this temperature, is very much higher.

Bread Making and Baking

Salt is added to make the bread more palatable; but it has also another effect. With inferior flour dextrin is formed inside the loaf to some extent as well as on the outside, consequently bread made from inferior flour rises badly and is darker in colour. This inferior flour is made sometimes from wheat that has been damp, the dampness causing the soluble albumenoids which the grain contains to act on the insoluble gluten, decomposing it into soluble bodies, and producing dextrin by their action on the starch in the grain. The further decomposition of these albumenoids is checked by the action of the salt during the fermentation of the bread.

And now it will be well to say something about the leaven of bread. We have already seen the modern method of making a ferment with flour, potatoes, and brewer's yeast; but there are other substances which do not cause fermentation, and yet lighten the bread, such as the different baking powders, and the American *sal eratus*, a mixture of bi-carbonate of soda and salt. Carbonate of ammonia, which entirely evaporates in baking, is used in confectionery to raise the paste by the bubbles it forms in its volatilisation. The unfermented breads, such as those made by the late Dr. Dauglish's patent (of which more anon), are rendered light upon the same principle, the usual method being to mix soda with the flour, and hydrochloric acid with the water, in the proportions in which they unite to form chloride of sodium, or common salt. The effervescence, like that produced in mixing seidlitz powders, converts the paste into a porous sponge, which, however, requires to be very quickly placed in the oven. The salt formed by the mixture replaces that ordinarily added to the dough in making bread; but this method is seldom used by practical bakers. Whatever, therefore, be the method by which bread is made light, the object to be attained is to pervade the dough with numerous cavities, which keep the particles of flour asunder, instead of forming a compact and unyielding mass.

The science which gave an insight into the cause of the 'rising' of bread, and suggested substitutes for the ordinary fermenting materials, is but of recent date. These ferments operate by generating an infinity of gas bubbles, which honeycomb the dough. The earliest process was to employ leaven, which is still largely used in the manufacture of the black rye bread of the Continent, and consists of dough which has become more or less sour by over-fermentation. This is kept from one baking to another, to inoculate a fresh bulk of paste with its fermenting influence. No sooner does it come into contact with the fresh dough than it communicates its own properties, as by contagion. Probably the discovery of leavening has, in many countries, been owing to accident, through neglected paste having been attacked by the fungus which is the cause of fermentation.

Many of my readers probably do not know that yeast is a plant. It belongs to the class of *fungi*, and, in accordance with the general habit of its kind, it differs from the green forms of vegetable life by feeding upon organic substances. The yeast plant represents one condition of a species of fungus re-

Bread Making and Baking

narkable for the diversity of forms it exhibits, its wide, nay, universal distribution, and the magnitude of the effects, sometimes beneficial, sometimes mischievous, which it is capable of producing. The forms in which it is familiar to most persons, although its nature may be unsuspected, are yeast, the gelatinous vinegar plant, the 'mother' of vinegar, and many decomposing vegetable infusions, and the common blue or green mould (*penicillium glaucum*) which occurs everywhere on sour paste, decaying fruits, and, in general, on all dead organic matters exposed to combined moisture and moderate heat.

Yeast and the vinegar plant are the forms in which it vegetates under various circumstances when well supplied with food. Mildew is its fruit, formed on the surfaces exposed to air at certain epochs, like the flowers and seeds of the higher plants, to enable it to diffuse itself, which it does most effectually, for the microscopic germs, invisible singly to the naked eye, are produced in myriads, and are so diminutive that ordinary motes floating in the atmosphere are large in comparison.

Yeast, when examined under the microscope, is found to consist of globular vesicles about $\frac{1}{2500}$th part of an inch in diameter when fully grown. They are multiplied by little vesicles budding out from the sides of the parent. These soon acquire an equal size, and repeat the reproduction, either while attracted to the parent globule or after separating from it. The multiplication goes on to an indefinite extent with a fitting supply of food and at a moderately warm temperature (70 deg.—90 deg. Fahr.). The vesicles

The History of Bread

are nourished by sucking in a portion of the organic liquid in which they exist, decomposing this chemically, and either actually giving off, or causing the separation of their outer surface, of carbonic acid in the form of gas. To give a familiar illustration of the action of the carbonic acid which is evolved from yeast on the dough, I may say that it is analogous to the froth formed on a tumbler of bottled ale or ginger-beer. The cavities or bubbles in the dough are produced in an exactly similar manner ; but two circumstances occur in bread to render them permanent—first, the fact that they are slowly formed ; secondly, that they are generated in a substance which, while it is soft enough to allow the bubbles to expand, is tough enough to retain them.

There are several kinds of yeast besides barm, or brewer's yeast, which, in spite of its bitter taste, is generally used by bakers because it is the least expensive. Next in consumption is what is termed press yeast, in German *press hefe* or *pfund hefe*, commonly known in commerce as German yeast, so called because it originally was a monopoly of that country, but it is now largely manufactured in Scotland. Of these yeasts Mr. Austin says :

'Press yeast is obtained partly by the brewing of beer or distillation of spirits as a by-product, partly it is made artificially. In the former case, the beer upper yeast is mixed with ten times its quantity of water, to which one per cent. of carbonate of ammonia is added, macerated and well washed for an hour, and then mixed with a compound of two parts

Bread Making and Baking

,f finely-powdered malt and ten parts starch, so that
ve have a firm mass, which is made into cakes half-
.n-inch thick. This yeast must be made fresh every
wo or three days, and must be kept in a cool place.
A better press yeast is made from the yeast of the
listilleries. The pasty residue of the mash tub is
)assed through a hair sieve to get rid of the grain
iusks. The filtrate is allowed to settle, and the
ediment is put into linen cloths and washed with
vater, and the water squeezed out again under gentle
)ressure. The yeast is thus obtained in the form of
·akes.'

Very many people prefer to make their own bread
nstead of buying it from the baker ; not that there is
. great saving, but there is a certain satisfaction in
:nowing by whom it is made, and as, doubtless, many
)f my readers have never attempted to make and
)ake their own bread, I venture to give Miss Acton's
very plain directions to a quite inexperienced learner
or making bread.'[1]

'If you have never yet attempted to make bread,
.nd wish to try to do it well, and have nobody to
how you the proper manner of setting about it, you
nay yet succeed perfectly by attending with great
:xactness to the directions which are given here; but,
s a large baking is less easily managed than a small
ne quite at first, and as the loss would be greater
: the bread were spoiled, I would advise you to begin
rith merely a loaf or two.

'Take, then, let us say, half a gallon of flour, or a

[1] *The English Bread Book for Domestic Use, &c.*, by Eliza Acton.
ondon, 1857. 8vo.

quartern, as it is called in some places. This will weigh three pounds and a half, and will make two loaves of nearly two pounds and a quarter each. There are two ways of making the dough, either of which, in experienced hands, will generally be attended with success. The most common mode of proceeding is to mix the yeast carefully with part of the liquid required for the whole of the bread, and to stir it into the centre of the flour; then to add by degrees what more of the liquid may be necessary, and to convert the whole with thorough, steady kneading into a firm but flexible paste, which, after standing in a suitable place until it has swollen to nearly double its original size, is again thoroughly kneaded, and once more left to "rise" or become porous before it is moulded into loaves and despatched to the oven.

'*To Make Dough by Setting a Sponge.*—This method of making dough is usually followed when there is any doubt either of the goodness or of the sufficient quantity of the yeast which is used for it, because if it should not become light after standing a certain time, more yeast, mixed with a little warm liquid, can easily be added to it, and the chance of having heavy bread be thus avoided.

'If you are sure of the goodness of the yeast you use it will not much matter which of them you follow. The quickest and easiest mode is to wet it up at once; the safest to guard against failure is to set a sponge thus: Put the flour into a large earthenware bowl or deep pan, then with a strong metal or wooden spoon hollow out the middle, but do not clear it entirely

Bread Making and Baking

away from the bottom of the pan, as in that case the sponge (or leaven as it was formerly termed) would stick to it, which it ought not to do. Next take either a large tablespoonful of brewer's yeast, which has been rendered solid by mixing it with cold water and letting it afterwards stand to settle for a day and a night, or nearly an ounce of fresh German yeast. Put it into a large basin and then proceed to mix it, so that it shall be as smooth as cream, with three-quarters of a pint or even a whole pint of just warm milk and water or water only, though even a very little milk will much improve the bread. To have it quite free from lumps you must pour in the liquid by spoonfuls just at the beginning, and stir and work it round well to mix it perfectly with the yeast before you add the remainder, otherwise it would probably cause the bread to be full of large holes, which ought never to be seen in it. Pour the yeast into the hole in the middle of the flour, and stir into it as much of that which lies around it as will make a thick batter, in which, remember, there must be no lumps. If there should seem to be any you must beat them out with the spoon. Strew plenty of flour on the top, throw a thick clean cloth over, and set it where the air is warm ; but if there is a large fire do not place it upon the kitchen fender in front of it, as servants often do, for it will become too much heated there ; but let it always be raised from the floor, and protected from constant draughts of air passing over it. Look at it from time to time when it has been laid for nearly an hour, and when you perceive that the yeast has risen and broken through the flour, and that bubbles appear in it, you will know that it is ready to be made up into dough. Then place the pan on a strong chair or dresser, or table of convenient height ; pour into the sponge a little warm milk and water (about a pint and a quarter will be required altogether for the quartern of bread), so that if three-quarters of a pint was mixed with the yeast at first there will be half a pint to add. Sometimes a little more will be needed ; but be always careful not to make the dough too moist ; stir into it as much flour as you can with the spoon, then wipe it out clean with your fingers and lay it aside.

'Next take plenty of the remaining flour, throw it on the top of the leaven, and begin with the knuckles of both hands to knead it well. Quick movement in this will do no good. It is strong, steady kneading which is required. Keep throwing up the flour which lies under and round the dough on to the top of it, that it may not stick to your fingers. You should always try to prevent its doing this, for you will soon discover that attention to these small particulars will make a great difference in the quality of your bread and in the time required to make it. When the flour is nearly all kneaded in begin to draw the edges of the dough towards the middle, in order to mix the whole thoroughly, and continue to knead it in every part, spreading it out, and then turning it constantly from the side of the pan to the middle, and pressing the knuckles of your closed hands well into and over it. When the whole of the flour is worked in, and the outside of the dough is free from it and from all lumps and crumbs, and does not stick to the hands when touched, it will be done, and may be again covered with the cloth and left to rise a second time.

'In three-quarters of an hour look at it, and should it have swollen very much, and begin to crack, it will be light enough to bake. Turn it then on to a paste-board, or very clean dresser, and, with a large sharp knife, divide it into two, when, if it has been carefully and properly made, you will find it full throughout of small holes like a fine sponge. When it is thus far ready make it up quickly into loaves, and despatch it to the oven. If it is to be baked in a flat tin or on the oven floor, dust a little flour on the board, and make them up lightly in the form of dumplings, drawing together the parts which are cut, and turning them downwards. Give them a good shape by working them round quickly between your hands without raising them from the board, and pressing them slightly as you do so; then take a knife in the right hand, and, turning each loaf quickly with the left, just draw the edge of it round the middle of the dough, but do not cut deeply into it; make also two or three slight incisions across the tops of the loaves, as they will rise more easily when this is done.

'Should it be put into earthen pans, the dough must be cut with the *point* of the knife just below the edge of the dishes after it is laid into them. To prevent it sticking to them, and being turned out with difficulty after it is baked, the pans should be rubbed in every part with a morsel of butter laid on a bit of clean paper. When they are only floured, the loaves cannot sometimes be loosened from these without being broken. All bread should be turned upside down or on its side as soon as it is drawn from the oven; if this be neglected, the under part of the loaves will become wet and blistered from the steam, which cannot then escape from them. They should remain until they are perfectly cold before they are put away and covered down.

'The only difference between this and the other way of making dough, mentioned at the beginning of these directions, is the mixing all the flour at first with the yeast and liquid into a firm smooth paste, which must be thoroughly kneaded down when it has become quite light, and then left to rise a second time before it is prepared for baking. A pint of warm milk and water, or of water only, may be stirred gradually to the yeast, which should then be poured into the middle of the flour, and worked with it into a stiff batter with a spoon, which should then be withdrawn, and the kneading with the hands commenced. Until a little experience has been gained, the mass of dough which will be formed with the pint of liquid, may be lifted from the pan into a dish, while sufficient warm water is added to wet up the remainder of the flour. This should afterwards be perfectly mingled with that which contains the yeast. A better plan is to use at once from a pint and a quarter to a pint and a half of liquid; but learners are very apt to pour in heedlessly more than is required, or to be inexact in the measure, and then more flour has to be used to make the bread of a proper consistence than is allowed for by the proportion of yeast named in the receipt. It is a great fault in bread-making to have the dough so moist that it sticks to the fingers when touched, and cannot be formed into loaves which will retain their shape without much flour being kneaded into them when they are made up for the oven.

'When it is to be *home baked* as well as home made, you must endeavour to calculate correctly the time at which it will be ready, and have the oven in a fit state for it when it is so. Should it have to be carried to the baker's, let a thick cloth or two be thrown over it before it is sent.'

In these very plain directions I do not find that Miss Acton specifies the quantity of salt to be used. Some, however, is absolutely necessary, to make good bread—say half an ounce to a quartern of flour.

CHAPTER XI.

OVENS ANCIENT AND MODERN.

WE have now got the loaf made, and the next thing is to bake it ; for the home-baked loaf, the oven of a kitchener or gas stove will do very well, and the heat should be about 400 deg. Fahr. A baker's oven is a thing *per se*. For hundreds of years they were made on the same old pattern, but now, except in many of the small underground bakeries, they are scientifically built, fitted with pyrometers, and with internal lamps Mr. Austin writes thus of the oven :

'The baker's oven is generally a brick oven, heated thoroughly with coal or wood according to construction ; if made for coal, the damper will be on the one side and the furnace on the other, so that the flames play all round the oven ; if constructed for wood, it must be heated with a good solid heat, with wood burnt in the interior of the oven, and then well cleaned out with a scuffle. As to the degrees of heat of the oven the laborious explanations and number of them may be reduced to three—viz., sharp or "flash," as named in recipes ; the second degree, moderate or "solid," as used for large or solid articles, as wedding cakes, &c. ; then slack or cool.

'The baker's old-fashioned method of testing the temperature of his oven is instructive. He throws flour on the floor. If it blackens without taking fire the heat is sufficient. It might be supposed that this is too high a temperature, as the object is to cook the bread, not to burn it ; but we must remember that the flour which has been prepared for baking is mixed with water, and the evaporation of this water will materially lower the temperature of the dough itself. Besides this, we must bear in mind that another object is to be attained. A hard shell or crust has been formed, which will so encase and support the lump of dough as to prevent it from subsiding when the further evolution, carbonic gas, shall cease, which will be the case some time before the cooking of the mass is completed. It will happen when the temperature reaches the point at which the yeast cells can no longer germinate, when the temperature is below the boiling point of water.

‘ In spite of all this outside temperature, that of the inner part of the loaf is kept down to a little above 212 degrees by the evaporation of the water contained in the bread ; the escape of this vapour and the expansion of carbonic acid bubbles by heat increasing the porosity of the loaf. The outside being heated considerably above the temperature of the inner part, this variation produces the difference between the crust and the crumb. The action of the high temperature indirectly converting some of the starch into dextrin will be understood from what is already stated, and also the partial conversion of this dextrin into caramel. Thus we have in the crust an excess of dextrin as compared with the crumb, and the addition of a variable quantity of caramel. In lightly baked bread, with the crust of uniform pale yellowish colour,

The History of Bread

the conversion of the dextrin into caramel has barely commenced, and the gummy character of the dextrin coating is well displayed. So much bread, especially the long staves of life common in France, appears as though they had been varnished, and their crust is partially soluble in water. This explains the apparent paradox that hard crust or dry toast is more easily digested than the soft crumb of bread, the cookery of the crumb not having been carried beyond the mere hydration of the gluten and the starch and such degree of dextrin formation as was due to the action of the diastaste of grain during the preliminary period of " rising." '

A form of oven now much in vogue is borrowed from Vienna. It is built of stone or brick; the roof is very low, and the floor slopes upwards towards the far end. The effect of this form of construction is to drive the steam rising from the loaves down on to the top of them again, thereby giving them the glazed surface so much admired in foreign bread. Steam is sometimes driven in with the same object; being lighter than that rising from the bread, it drives the latter down. The ovens are heated from below. Loaves remain in for one and a half or two hours.

As in everything connected with baking, during the past few years great improvements have been made in bakers' ovens. Science has been brought to bear upon them, and we now have them heated by gas or steam in addition to coal and coke, besides improved alterations in many ways.

Nor do modern improvements in baking appliances stop short at ovens. Most bakers doing a good business use kneading machines, of which there are many in the market. With one exception—that of the Adair mixer, which has no arms nor beaters, but simply rotates, and by this action the flour and water pass through the rods of iron, which are placed crosswise in the machine, and become perfectly and proportionately mixed—they are all, more or less, on the same principle, of revolving arms, blades, or knives by which the flour and water are properly mixed, and the position of the dough being perpetually changed, it is effectually kneaded without the objectionable intervention of manual labour.

The earliest kneading machine that I can find mentioned is in 1850, when the illustrious philosopher, Arago, presented and recommended to the Institute of France the kneading and baking apparatus of M. Rolland, then a humble baker of the Twelfth Arrondissement. The kneading machine was described as exceedingly simple, and capable of being worked, when under a full charge, by a young man from 15 to 20 years old, the necessity for horse labour or steam power being thus obviated ; and it was claimed that in less than twenty minutes a sack of flour could be converted into a perfect homogeneous and aerated dough altogether superior to any dough that could be obtained by manual kneading.

Another attempted improvement in the manufacture of bread was aerating the dough without using any ferment, such as yeast, etc., and this has been accomplished by means of mixing hydrochloric acid and carbonate of soda with the dough, or using bicarbonate of ammonia, or forcing carbonic acid into the water with which the flour is mixed. The latter is called the Dauglish system, from its inventor, the late John Dauglish, M.D. (born 1824, died January 14, 1866), and it is now in full working operation.

By this system carbonic acid gas is generated as if for making soda water, and, supposing a sack of flour was to be converted into dough, the following would be the treatment: A lid at the top of the mixer is opened, and the flour passed down into it through a spout from the floor above. The lid of the mixer is then fitted tightly on, and the air within it exhausted by the pump. The requisite quantity of water, about 17 gallons, is drawn into the water vessel, and carbonic acid is forced into it till the pressure amounts to from 15lb. to 25lb. per square inch. The aerated water is then passed into the mixer, and the mixing arms are set in motion, by which, in about seven minutes, the flour and water are incorporated into a perfectly uniform paste. At the lower end of the mixer a cavity is arranged, gauged to hold sufficient dough for a 2lb. loaf, and by a turn of a lever that quantity is dropped into a pan ready for at once depositing in the oven. The whole of the operations can be performed in less than half an hour.

The advantages of this system are absolute purity and cleanliness, but it is simply porous dough, and has not got the flavour of fermented bread. The plant, too, is very expensive, which renders it impossible for the ordinary baker to adopt it.

Certainly, machinery has been applied with very great advantage to the manufacture of another kind of bread, on which they that go down upon the sea in ships were wont to depend—namely, ship's biscuits. Badly made of bad materials, and ofttimes full of weevils were they, so hard that they had to be soaked in some liquid before they could be eaten, or else broken up and boiled with the pea soup.

Up to the year 1833 the ships of the Royal Navy were supplied with biscuits made at Gosport by gangs of five men, severally named the *furner*, the *mate*, the *driver*, the *brakeman*, and the *idleman*. The *driver* made the dough in a trough with his naked arms. The rough dough was then placed on a wooden platform, to be worked by the *brakeman*, who kneaded it by riding and jumping on it. Then it was taken to a moulding board, cut into slips, moulded by hand, docked, or pierced full of holes, and pitched into the oven by the joint action of the gang. The nine ovens in the Royal Clarence Victualling Yard required the labour of 45 men to keep them in full operation, and the product was about 14cwt. of biscuit per hour, at a cost for labour and utensils of 1*s* 7*d.* per cwt. This system was superseded by machinery, and biscuits have been for many years past produced with almost incredible rapidity, perfect in kneading, moulding, and baking, and at a cost for labour and utensils of less than a third of the old outlay.

CHAPTER XII.

THE RELIGIOUS USE OF BREAD.

OF the many breads that are not in common use, that used in the celebration of the Communion should be placed first. There seems no room for doubt that, at the Last Supper, our Lord broke unleavened bread—St. Luke xxii. is, apparently, conclusive on this point ; and, to this day, the whole Latin, Armenian, and Maronite Churches use unleavened bread, and it is also used in many churches of the Anglican communion. Dr. Lee [1] says : ' The Ethiopic Christians also use unleavened bread at their Mass on Maundy Thursday, but leavened bread on other occasions. The Greek and other Oriental Churches use leavened bread, which is especially made for the purpose, with scrupulous care and attention. The Christians of St. Thomas likewise make use of leavened bread, composed of fine flour, which, by an ancient rule of theirs, ought to be prepared on the same day upon which it is to be consecrated. It is circular in shape, stamped with a large cross, the border being edged with smaller crosses, so that, when it is broken up, each fragment may contain the holy symbol. In the Roman Catholic Church the bread is made thin and circular, and bears upon it either the impressed figure

---

[1] *A Glossary of Liturgical and Ecclesiastical Terms.* By the Rev. F. G. Lee. London : 1877 ; p. 17.

The Religious Use of Bread

of the crucifix, or the letters I.H.S. Pope St. Zephyrinus, who lived in the third century, terms the Sacramental bread, *Corona sive oblata, sphericæ, figuræ*, "a crown, or oblation, of a spherical figure," the circle being indicative of the Divine presence after consecration. The Orientals, occasionally, make their altar breads square, on which is stamped a cross, with an inscription. The square form of the bread is a mystical indication that, by the sacrifice of Christ upon the cross, salvation is purchased for the four corners of the earth.' And Dr. Lee gives illustrations of the altar bread, or wafers, in use in the Latin, Armenian, Coptic, and Greek Churches.

It seems certain that, in the Primitive Church, neither unleavened bread nor wafers were used. Ancient writers say that the bread used was common bread, such as was made for their own use. It was also a charge against the Ebionites that they celebrated in unleavened bread and water only. The bread generally used was called *fermentum*, and though this is explained by the schoolmen, who claimed primitive custom for unleavened bread, as the *eulogia*, or *panis benedictus*, which was blessed for such as did not communicate, Pope Innocent I. plainly says that it refers to the Sacrament itself. Moreover, no Greek writer before Michael Cerularius, who lived A.D. 1051, objected to the use of unleavened bread in the Roman Church, which would seem to show that it was not extensively used before that time. Even some Roman writers speak of the custom as erroneous.

How the change in this matter was made, and the

The History of Bread

exact time when, is not easily determined. Cardinal Bona's conjecture seems probable enough : that it crept in when the people began to leave off making their oblations in common bread. This occasioned the clergy to provide it themselves, and they, under pretence of decency and respect, brought it from leaven to unleaven, and from a loaf of common bread, that might be broken, to a nice and delicate wafer, formed in the figure of a *denarius*, or penny, to represent the pence for which our Saviour was betrayed ; and then, also, the people, instead of offering a loaf of bread, as formerly, were ordered to offer a penny, which was either to be given to the poor, or to be expended upon something pertaining to the sacrifice of the altar.

The alteration in the Communion bread occasioned great disputes between the Eastern and Western Churches.

The first Common Prayer Book of Edward VI. enjoins unleavened bread to be used throughout the whole kingdom for the celebration of the Eucharist. It was ordered to be *round,* in imitation of the wafers used in the Greek and Roman Churches ; but it was to be *without all manner of print,* the wafers usually having the impression either of a crucifix or the Holy Lamb ; and *something more large and thicker* than the wafers, which were the size of a penny. This rubric, affording matter for scruple, was set aside at the review of the Liturgy, in the fifth year of King Edward ; and another inserted in its room, which still exists, by which it is declared sufficient that *the bread be such as is usually eaten.*

The Religious Use of Bread

It was the custom in Westminster Abbey, and in the Royal chapels, and the practice of such men as Bishop Andrewes, to use wafers, but 'for peace sake,' where wafers were objected to, plain and pure wheaten bread was allowed. It has been decided by the Privy Council that it not only may, but must, be common bread; the Injunctions, according to them, being of no validity against the rubric; while the Advertisements, having been made under Act of Parliament, and not contrary to the rubric, are an indication of its meaning—*i.e.*, of the word 'retained in the Ornaments rubric.'

The bread now used is common wheaten bread in most Protestant Churches. In some Presbyterian Churches a special kind of wafer is prepared for the purpose. In the Roman Church thin wafers are used. In the Eastern Churches they are of different sizes and thicknesses.

They are thus classified by the Rev. F. E. Brightman in *Liturgies Eastern* :

1. Byzantine; a round leavened cake 5 × 2 in., stamped with a square (2 in.); itself divided by a cross into four squares in which are severally inscribed IC, XC, NI, KA.

2. The Syrian Jacobite and Syrian Uniat; a round cake, leavened with the holy leaven, 3 × ¾, stamped like a wheel with four diameters (the alternate radii being cut off half way from the circumference by a concentric circle).

3. The Marionite ; the Latin unleavened wafer.

4. The Coptic ; a round leavened cake, 3½ × ¾, stamped round the edge with the legend, Αγιος οθεος,

αγιος ισχυρος, αγιος αθανατος, and within with a cross consisting of twelve little squares, each of which and the remaining spandrels are marked with a little cross placed diagonally.

5. The Abyssinian ; a flat round leavened cake, 4 × ¾, stamped with a cross of nine squares with four squares added in the angles of the cross.

6. The Nestorian ; a round leavened cake, 2 × ½, stamped with a cross-crosslet and four small crosses.

7. The Armenian ; a round unleavened wafer, 3 × ⅛, stamped with an ornamental border, the crucifix and the sacred name and sometimes with two diameters at right angles to the back.

In regard to the Protestant Non-Episcopal Churches, it is stated in Herzog's *Religious Encyclopædia* that the administration follows one of two types. These are the Lutheran and the Calvinistic. In the Lutheran, the elements are consecrated with the sign of the cross, a wafer of unleavened bread is given whole to the communicant, and white wine, instead of red, is used. The communicants kneel and receive the elements into their mouths instead of their hands. The Calvinistic type simplifies the service as much as possible, and assimilates it to a common meal. 'In the French Reformed Church the elements are placed —the bread in two silver dishes, and the wine in two silver cups—on a table spread with a white linen cloth. From twenty-five to thirty communicants approach the table at a time. The officiating minister makes a free prayer, and then, while repeating the words of institution, presents the elements to his neighbours on the left and on the right, after which the dish and the cup pass from hand to hand. With various modifications this type has been adopted by all the Reformed (Non-Episcopal) Churches.'

This is practically the method adopted in most of the British Non-Episcopal Churches ; instead, however, of the communicants coming forward to the table, they remain in their pews, the bread and wine being handed round by elders or deacons. In the American Non-Episcopal Churches the same plan is usually adopted.

These divergencies of method illustrate the strange fact in the Christian life, that around the simple and beautiful institution of the Lord's Supper there have raged the fiercest controversies in religious history. So divergent are the views held about it, that the Roman Catholic Church asserts that in every celebration of the Mass our Saviour is again actually offered as a sacrifice, and the bread and wine become the actual body and blood of the Lord, this miracle of transformation being wrought through the consecrating prayer of the priest. The Quakers, at the other extreme, do not observe the service at all, and do not consider it to be a binding ordinance. Here, as so often in life, the truth lies between the extremes. The bread and the wine are the symbols of our Lord's body and blood. We do not feed on Him by the mere physical eating of the consecrated elements, but we partake of Him through faith as we remember that His body was broken for us, and His blood shed for the remission of our sins. His own loving command as He sat at the table with His disciples was, 'This do in remembrance of Me,' and it is

The History of Bread

through fellowship with Him in spirit—in the Garden of Gethsemane and on the cross at Calvary—that 'we feed on Him in our hearts by faith with thanksgiving.'

There is a semi-sacred bread eaten by the English race, and by no one else—the hot-cross bun—millions of which are devoured in England on Good Friday. Its origin is obscure, as is also that of the word 'bun.' Most dictionaries derive it from the old French *bigne*, or *bugne*—a swelling; but it certainly occurs in an early *Promptorium Parvulorum*, as 'bunne-brede.' Anent 'Eating Buns on Good Friday,' a correspondent in the *Athenæum* of April 4, 1857, p. 144, wrote:

'In the *Museo Lapidario* of the Vatican, on the Christian side of it, and not far off from the door leading into the library, there is a tablet representing in a rude manner the miracle of the five barley loaves. Every visitor must have seen it, for it has been there for years. The loaves are round, like cakes, and have a cross upon them, such as our cakes bear, which are broken and eaten on Good Friday morning, symbolical of the sacrifice of the body of our Lord. Five of these cakes, explanatory of the scene, are ranged beneath an arch-shaped table, at which recline five people, while another, with a basket full, is occupied in serving them. The cakes are so significant of the Bread of Life that one might almost regard the repast as intended to prefigure the sacrifice that was to follow, and the institution connected with it. Having, from the earliest period of memory, cherished a particular regard for hot-cross buns and

The Religious Use of Bread

all their pleasing associations, it was a source of gratifying reflection to see my old favourites thus brought into intimate association with the pious thoughts of the primitive Christians, and to know that at home we cherished an ancient usage on Good Friday which the more Catholic nations of Europe no longer observed. But, alas! there is always some drawback to our full satisfaction in this world, and knowledge is often a cruel dissipation of favourite convictions; my faith in the Christian biography of these buns has recently received a very rude shock.

'It would appear that they have descended to us, not from any Popish practice, as some *pious* souls affirm, but from one which was actually, and, like the word which we use to signify the great festival of the Church, *Easter*, to a paganism as ancient as the worship of *Astarte*, in honour of whom, about the time of the Passover, our pagan ancestors, the Saxons, baked and offered up a particular kind of cake. We read in Jeremiah (vii. 17, 18): "Seest thou not what they do in the cities of Judah and in the streets of Jerusalem? The children gather wood, and the fathers kindle the fire, and the women knead their dough, to make cakes to the Queen of Heaven." [See also Jeremiah xliv. 18, 19.] Dr. Stukeley, in his *Medallic History of Valerius Carausius*, remarks that they were "assiduous to knead the Easter cakes for her service." The worship of a Queen of Heaven, under some significant name or other, was an almost universal practice, and exists still in various parts of the globe. She is usually represented, like the Madonna, bearing her son in her lap, or like Isis, with

149

the infant Horus. We may see such images in the Louvre, and in the great Ethnographical Museum at Copenhagen, where the Queen of Heaven of the Chinese, *Tien-how*, figures in white porcelain, side by side with *Schling-mu*, the Holy Mother. Certain metaphysical ideas are apt to flow in a common channel, and get clothed in the same symbolical dress. Hence we find a Queen of Heaven, no less in Mexico than in China, in Egypt, Greece, Italy, and England; and, under the pagan title of a Christian festival, preserve, along with our buns, the memorial of her ancient reign.'

CHAPTER XIII.

GINGER BREAD AND CHARITY BREAD.

BUT there is a bread which must not escape notice
—a true bread—although somewhat sweet and spiced.
When it was first introduced into England no one can
tell, but it was well known in the reign of Queen
Elizabeth, for Shakespeare, in *Love's Labour Lost*
(Act v., s. 1), makes Costard say : 'An I had but
one penny in the world, thou shouldst have it to buy
gingerbread.' And we find it used in a similar way
to the educational biscuits of the present day ; for
Matthew Prior, in his *Alma* says :

> ' To Master John, the English maid
> A horn-book gives, of gingerbread ;
> And, that the child may learn the better,
> As he can name, he eats the letter.'

It was made with honey, before the introduction
of sugar, and must be of remote antiquity and inti-
mately allied to our friend the *Bous*. The Rhodians
made bread with honey which was so pleasant that it
was eaten as cake after dinner. The German gingerbread and the French *pain d'épice* used both to be
made with honey. The use of gingerbread is widely
spread, and wherever it is eaten it is popular, even
in the far East Indies, where both natives and Anglo-
Indians rejoice in it. In Holland it is in more request
than in any other country in Europe, and the recipe

The History of Bread

for its manufacture is guarded as a jealous secret and descends as an heirloom from father to son.

In its early days gingerbread was an unleavened cake, and the first attempt to make it light was to

introduce pearl-ash or potash; afterwards alum was introduced, now it is made of ordinary fermented dough, or with carbonate of ammonia. When well made, gingerbread will last good for years; but if not well made, and of good materials, it will last no time,

Ginger Bread and Charity Bread

but will get soft with the first damp weather. Such was the stuff sold at fairs—both thick gingerbread and nuts—booths being erected for the sale of nothing else. The background of these booths was ornamented by gingerbread crowns, kings and queens, cocks, etc., dazzlingly resplendent with *pseudo* gold leaf, or, as it was then called, 'Dutch metal.' I do not think that anybody ever ate any of these works of art, I think they were solely for ornament; and, when combined with bows and streamers of bright-coloured ribbons, they made the gingerbread booths the most attractive in the fair.

In the last century it was a great institution, and Swift, writing to Stella, says : ''Tis a loss you are not here, to partake of three weeks' frost, and eat ginger-bread in a booth by a fire on the Thames.' There was a famous itinerant vendor of this article named Ford, but who was more generally known as 'Tiddy Diddy Doll,' from a song he used to sing whose words were but those. He flourished in the middle of last century, and Hogarth painted him in one of the scenes of 'Industry and Idleness,' where the idle apprentice is going to his doom.

Hone, in his *Every Day Book*, vol. i., p. 375, etc., gives a very good account of Ford. He says : 'This celebrated vendor of gingerbread, from his eccentricity of character, and extensive dealings in his way, was always hailed as the king of itinerant tradesmen.[1] In his person he was tall, well made, and his features handsome. He affected to dress like a person of rank—white and gold suit of clothes,

[1] He was a constant attendant in the crowds at Lord Mayor's Day.

HOGARTH'S PICTURE OF FORD.

154

Ginger Bread and Charity Bread

laced ruffled shirt, laced hat and feathers, white silk stockings, with the addition of a fine white apron. Among his harangues to gain customers, take this as a specimen: 'Mary, Mary, where are you now, Mary? I live, when I am at home, at the second house in Little Ball Street, two steps underground, with a wiscum, riscum, and a why-not. Walk in, ladies and gentlemen, my shop is on the second floor backwards, with a brass knocker at the door. Here's your nice gingerbread, your spice gingerbread; it will melt in your mouth like a red-hot brick-bat, and rumble in your inside like Punch and his wheelbarrow.' . . . . For many years (and perhaps at present) allusion was made to his name, as thus: 'You are so fine, you look like Tiddy Doll. You are as tawdry as Tiddy Doll. You are quite Tiddy Doll,' etc.

But there is a use for badly-made gingerbread which perhaps some of us do not know—a gingerbread barometer. It is nothing more than the figure of a General made of gingerbread, which Clavette buys every year at the *Place du Trone*. When he gets home he hangs his purchase on a nail. You know the effect of the atmosphere on gingerbread; the slightest moisture renders it soft; in dry weather, on the contrary, it grows hard and tough. Every morning, on going out, Clavette asks his servant, 'What does the General say?' The man forthwith applies his thumb to the figure, and replies, 'The General feels flabby about the chest; you'd better take your umbrella!' On the other hand, when the symptoms are hard and unyielding, our worthy colleague sallies forth in his new hat.

A curious use of dough, somewhat sweetened, was made at Christmas, when it was manufactured into *Yule doughs*, or dows, or *Yule babies*, small images like dolls with currants for eyes, intended probably to represent the infant Jesus, which were presented by bakers to the children of their customers. Another Christmas custom connected with dough used to obtain in Wiltshire, where a hollow loaf, containing an apple, and ornamented on the top with the head of a cock or a dragon, with currant eyes, and made of paste, was baked, and put by a child's bedside on Christmas morning to be eaten before breakfast. This was called a *Cop-a-loaf*, or *Cop-loaf*.

Much land in England was held by tenure, in which bread plays a part, as the following instances out of many will show.[1]

Apelderham, Sussex.—John Aylemer holds by court roll one messuage and one yard [thirty acres] land . . . And he ought to find at three reap days, in autumn, every day, two men, and was to have for each of the said men, on every of such reap days, viz., on each of the two first days, one loaf of wheat and barley mixed, weighing eighteen pounds of wax, every loaf to be of the price of a penny farthing ; and at the third reap day each man was to have a loaf of the same weight, all of wheat, of the price of a penny halfpenny.

Chakedon, Oxon.—Every mower on this manor

---

[1] *Tenures of Land and Customs of Manors*, originally collected by Thomas Blount. London, 1874, 8vo.

was to have a loaf of the price of a halfpenny, besides other things.

Glastonbury, Somerset.—In the thirty-third year of Edward I., William Pasturell held twelve ox-gangs of land there from the abbot, by service of finding a cook in the kitchen of the said abbot and a baker for the bakehouse.

Hallaton, Leicester.—A piece of land was bequeathed to the use and advantage of the rector, who was there to provide 'two hare pies, a quantity of ale, and two dozen of penny loaves, to be scrambled for on Easter Monday annually.'

Lenneston or Loston, Devon.—Geoffrey de Alba-Marlia held this hamlet of the King, rendering therefore to the King, as often as he should hunt in the Forest of Dartmoor, one loaf of oat bread of the value of half a farthing, and three barbed arrows, feathered with peacock's feathers, and fixed in the aforesaid loaf.

Liston, Essex.—In the forty-first year of Edward III., Nan, the wife of William Leston, held the manor of Overhall, in this parish, by the service of paying for, bringing in, and placing of five wafers before the King, as he sits at dinner, upon the day of his coronation.

Twickenham, Middlesex.—There was an ancient custom here of dividing two great cakes in the church among the young people on Easter Day ; but, it being looked upon as a superstitious relic, it was ordered by Parliament, in 1645, that the parishioners should forbear that custom, and instead thereof buy loaves of bread for the poor of the parish with the money that

The History of Bread

should have bought the cakes. It is probable that the cakes were bought at the vicar's expense ; for it appears that the sum of one pound per annum is still charged upon the vicarage for the purpose of buying penny loaves for poor children on the Thursday before Easter. Within the memory of man they were thrown from the church steeple to be scrambled for.

Wells, Dorset.—Richard de Wells held this manor ever since the Conquest by the service of being baker to our Lord the King.

Witham, Essex.—By an inquisition made in the reign of Henry III., it appears that one Geoffrey de Lyston held land at Witham by the service of carrying flour to make wafers on the King's birthday, whenever his Majesty was in the Kingdom.

Of bread, as given away in charity or by dole, the examples in England are almost numberless ; still a few somewhat redeemed from common place, and extracted from the Report on Charities, may interest the reader.[1]

Assington, Suffolk.—John Winterflood, by will dated April 2, 1593, gave to the poor of Assington four bushels of meslin (wheat and rye) payable out of the manor of Aveley Hall, to be distributed in bread at Christmas ; and four bushels of meslin, out of the rectory or priory of Assington, to be distributed in bread at Easter ; and under this donation four bushels of wheat are brought to Assington Church and distributed among the poor at Christmas, and the like quantity of wheat at Easter.

[1] *A Collection of Old English Customs, etc.* By H. Edwards. London, 1842.

Ginger Bread and Charity Bread

St. Bartholomew by the Exchange, London.—
Several benefactors have given bread to the poor
of this parish. Richard Crowshaw, goldsmith, by
will, April 26, 1531, directed that 100*l.* should
be paid to provide 2*s.* weekly for ever, to be laid

THE BIDDENDEN MAIDS.

out in good cheese, to be delivered to the poor
parishioners of this parish, according as they received
the bread, which then was and had been long given
them.

Another bread and cheese charity still obtains in
the village of Biddenden, Kent, about four miles from
Tenterden; and it is noticeable on account of the

159

The History of Bread

tradition which assigns its foundation to a *lusus naturæ* similar to the Siamese twins of our day. The founders of the charity, according to tradition, were Eliza and Mary Chulkhurst, who were born in 1100, and lived together, joined at hips and shoulders, for 34 years. To perpetuate their memory, biscuits, measuring 3½ in. by 2 in. and about ¼ in. thick, are made and distributed with the dole of bread on Easter Sunday. On these biscuits is stampèd a rude representation of the 'Biddenden Maids.' There are two moulds, one made of beech-wood, judging from the twins' costume of *commode*, or cap, and laced bodice, dates from the time of William and Mary or Anne ; the other, which is of boxwood, although an attempted copy, is undoubtedly more modern. The writer has the biscuits, and with them came the following paper, headed by a rough woodcut :

'A short and concise history of Eliza and Mary Chulkhurst, who were both joined together by the hips and shoulders, in the year of our Lord 1100, at Biddenden, in the County of Kent, commonly called " The Biddenden Maids." '

The reader will observe by the plate that they lived together in the above state 34 years, at the expiration of which time one of them was taken ill, and in a short time died ; the surviving one was advised to be separated from the body of her deceased sister by dissection, but she absolutely refused the separation by saying these words, 'As we came together we will also go together'; and in the space of about six hours after her sister's decease she was taken ill and died also.

Ginger Bread and Charity Bread

By their will they bequeathed to the churchwardens of the parish of Biddenden and their successor churchwardens, for ever, certain pieces or parcels of land in the parish of Biddenden, containing 20 acres, more or less, which are now let at 40 guineas per annum. There are usually made, in commemoration of these wonderful phenomena of Nature, about 1000 rolls (*sic*) with their impressions printed on them, and given away to all strangers on Easter Sunday, after Divine Service in the afternoon ; also about 500 quartern loaves, and cheese in proportion, to all the poor inhabitants of the said parish.

Hasted, in his *History of the County of Kent* (edit. 1790, Vol. III., p. 66), says, with regard to this benefaction : ' There is a vulgar tradition in these parts that the figures on the cakes represent the donors of this gift, being two women—twins—who were joined together in their bodies, and lived together so till they were between 20 and 30 years of age. But this seems without foundation. The truth seems to be that it was the gift of two maidens of the name of *Preston*, and that the print of the women on the cakes has only taken place within these 50 years, and was made to represent two poor widows, as the general objects of a charitable benefaction. *William Horner*, rector of this parish, in 1656, brought a suit in the Exchequer for the recovery of these lands, as having been given for an augmentation of his glebe land ; but he was nonsuited.'

CHAPTER XIV.

BREAD RIOTS.

BREAD riots are of comparatively modern date. In the olden days people suffered from scarcity, but they suffered without making senseless riots. There was no Free Trade in corn, and the people had to depend upon home-grown cereals; so that in times of drought or failure of crops they felt the pinch terribly. True, they had a certain amount of protection against overcharge and combination in the form of the Assize of Bread, which, while it gave the baker a working profit, gave the consumer the benefit of a sliding-scale according to the market value of wheat.

It is not worth while going very far back to write the history of hard times and how they were met; a hundred years is quite long enough for retrospect. Suffice it, then, that the years 1795–96 were years of great scarcity, and all classes, from the peasant to the King, felt it, and met it like men. To cope with this dearth, the best way seemed to them to diminish, as far as possible, the use of wheaten flour, and to provide substitutes therefor. The King set his subjects a good example.

'His Majesty has given orders for the bread used

in his household to be made of meal and rye mixed. No other sort is permitted to be baked, and the royal family eat bread of the same quality as their servants do. It is extremely sweet and palatable.

'One half flour, and half potatoes, also make a very excellent bread.' (*Times*, July 22, 1795.)

'The writer of this paragraph has seen the bread that is eaten at his Majesty's table. It consists of two sorts only, the one composed of wheaten flour and rye mixed ; the other is half wheaten flour, half potato flour. If ever example deserved imitation, it is this.' (*Times*, July 30, 1795.)

People were requested to discontinue the use of hair powder, which was made of starch obtained from wheat, and very many did so ; in fact, this movement extended to the Army, for we read in the *Times*, Feb. 10, 1795 : 'In consequence of the scarcity of wheat, arising partly from such quantities of it being used for hair powder, several regiments have, very patriotically, discontinued the use of hair powder, which, in these instances, was generally nothing but flour.'

Potatoes came very much to the fore as a substitute for wheat, and the Parliamentary Board of Agriculture proposed a premium of one thousand pounds to the person who would grow the largest breadth of potatoes on lands never before applied to the culture of that plant.

The City authorities watched the bakers narrowly as to short weight, and amerced them 5s. per ounce short, one man having to pay, with costs, £106 5s. on

The History of Bread

420 ounces deficient in weight. Wheat in August, 1795, was 13s. 6d. per bushel, and the price of the quartern loaf should then have been 1s. 6d., as it was 1s. 3d. in January, 1796, when wheat was 11s. 6d. per bushel. It fell rapidly after harvest, and in December, 1796, was 7s. 4d. per bushel. It must be remembered that money then had twice its present value.

In 1800 there was another scarcity, and in February of that year a Bill passed into law which enacted 'That it shall not be lawful for any baker, or other person, or persons, residing within the cities of London and Westminster, and the Bills of Mortality, and within ten miles of the Royal Exchange, after the 26th day of February, 1800, or residing in any part of Great Britain after the 4th day of March, 1800, to sell, or offer to expose for sale, any bread, until the same shall have been baked 24 hours at the least.'

The average price of wheat this year was 14s. 1d. per bushel, and in July, just before harvest, it rose to 16s. 10d. or 134s. 8d. per quarter, and other provisions were very dear. The people were less patient than in 1795–6, and in August and September several riots took place at Birmingham, Oxford, Nottingham, Coventry, Norwich, Stamford, Portsmouth, Sheffield, Worcester, and many other places. The markets were interrupted, and the populace compelled the farmers, etc., to sell their provisions at a low price.

At last these riots extended to London, beginning in a very small way. Late at night on Saturday, September 13, or early on Sunday, the 14th, two large, written placards were pasted on the Monument, the text of which was—

'Bread will be sixpence the quartern, if the people will assemble at the Corn Market on Monday.

'FELLOW COUNTRYMEN,

'How long will ye quietly and cowardly suffer your-selves to be imposed upon and half-starved by a set of mercenary slaves and Government hirelings? Can you still suffer them to proceed in their extensive monopolies while your children are crying for bread? No! let them not exist a day longer. We are the sovereignty; rise then from your lethargy. Be at the Corn Market on Monday.'

By means of these placards, and handbills to the same effect, a mob of over a thousand was collected in Mark Lane by nine a.m., and their number was doubled in another hour. They hissed and pelted the corn factors; but, about eleven a.m., when they began to break windows, the Lord Mayor appeared upon the spot. In vain he assured them that their behaviour could in no way affect the market. They only yelled at him, 'Cheap bread!' 'Birmingham and Nottingham for ever!' 'Three loaves for eighteen-pence,' etc. They even hissed the Lord Mayor and smashed the windows close by him. This was more than he could bear, and he ordered the Riot Act to be read. The constables charged the mob, who, of course, fled, and the Lord Mayor returned to the Mansion House.

They only went to other parts of the City, and,

The History of Bread

when night fell, they began smashing windows, etc.
At last, fear of their firing the City induced the
authorities to invoke the assistance of some Volunteers
and Militia, and by their efforts the mob was driven
over London Bridge into Southwark, where they
rendered the night lively by breaking windows, etc.

For a day or two there was peace; but on the
morning and during the day and night of the 18th of
September the mob had it all their own way, breaking windows and pillaging. A royal proclamation
was issued, calling on the civil authorities to suppress
these riots, which was done at last by means of
cavalry and Volunteers, but only after the mob having
two more days' uncontrolled possession of London.
But the people in the country were not so quickly
satisfied; their wages were smaller than those of
their London brethren, and they proportionately felt
the pinch more acutely. In some instances they
were put down by force, in others the price of bread
was lowered; but it is impossible at this time to
take up a newspaper and not find some notice of
or allusion to a food riot.

The importation of foreign corn supplied the
deficiency of the English crops, and bread was
moderately cheap; but in 1815, probably with a
view to assuage the agricultural distress then prevalent, a measure was proposed and passed by which
foreign corn was to be prohibited, except when wheat
had reached 80s. a quarter—a price considered by the
great body of consumers as exorbitant. A resolution
was passed 'That it is the opinion of the Committee
that any sort of foreign corn, meal, or flour, which

Bread Riots

may by law be imported into the United Kingdom shall at all times be allowed to be brought into the United Kingdom, and to be warehoused there, without payment of any duty whatever.'

The popular feeling was well worked on; and on March 6 groups of people assembled near the Houses of Parliament, about the usual time of meeting, hooting or cheering the members, and occasionally stopping a carriage and making its occupant walk through the crowd, which at last got so unruly that it was obliged to be dispersed by the military. Yet the whole night they were parading the streets, breaking windows, and yelling: 'No Corn Bill!' This conduct continued for two nights longer, until the rioters had almost worn themselves out, when an increase of military force finally extinguished the rising. But there were riots all over the country.

In 1828 an Act of Parliament was passed which fixed the duty on foreign wheat according to a 'sliding scale,' whereby it was diminished from 1l. 5s. 8d. per quarter whenever the average price of all England was under 62s., and was gradually reduced, as wheat rose in price, until the duty stood at 1s. when wheat was 73s. and upwards.

Great agitation prevailed as to free corn; and on September 18, 1838, the Anti-Corn Law League, for procuring the repeal of the laws charging duty upon the importation of corn, was founded at Manchester. This organisation lectured, harangued, distributed pamphlets, and was perpetually in evidence—and at last succeeded in its object.

The 5 Vict., c. 14 (April 29, 1842), was a revised

sliding scale. When wheat was under 51s. the duty to be 1l; when 73s. and over, 1s.; and this lasted until the Corn Importation Bill (9, 10, Vic., c. 22) was passed on June 26, 1846, which reduced the duty on wheat to 4s. when imported at or above 53s., until Feb. 1, 1849, when 1s. duty per quarter only was to be levied on all kinds of imported grain. This shilling was taken off on June 24, 1869, and there is now no hindrance of any sort to the importation of foreign corn.

Although there was fierce political contention over the Anti-Corn Law agitation physical force was not resorted to, and the next bread riots we hear of were in 1855. They seem to have begun at Liverpool, where, on Feb. 19, an unruly mob took possession of the city, clamouring for bread and looting the bakers' shops. The police were unable to cope with the riot; therefore, special constables were sworn in and peace was restored towards evening. Next day about 60 prisoners were brought before the magistrates; some were committed for trial, others sentenced to one, two, or three months' imprisonment.

The riot spread to London, and during the night of Feb. 21 and the whole day of Feb. 22 the East End and South of London were terrorised by bands of men perambulating the streets and demanding bread and money from the inhabitants; some shops were looted, but, thanks to the police and the distribution of a large quantity of bread, serious consequences were averted. Several arrests were made and punishment duly meted out.

On September 14, 1855, there were bread riots

Bread Riots

in Nottingham, where the mob broke the bakers'
windows and proceeded to such extremities that
special constables were sworn in and peace was
restored.

On three successive Sundays, October 14, 21, and
28, 1855, there were disorderly meetings on account
of the dearness of bread held in Hyde Park ; the
windows of many houses were smashed, but the
disturbances hardly amounted to riot ; and the same
occurred on November 4, 11, and 18, but the police
prevented the mob from doing much mischief. Since
then we have never known a *bread riot*, although the
unemployed, Anarchists, etc., have at times been
troublesome.

CHAPTER XV.

LEGENDS ABOUT BREAD.

As might be expected in an article of such world-wide consumption as bread, there is a considerable amount of folk-lore and sayings attendant on it. We can even find it in Shakespeare, for, in *Hamlet* (Act iv. s. 5), Ophelia says : 'They say the owl was a baker's daughter.' This, unless one knew the Gloucestershire legend, would be unintelligible, but the bit of folk-lore makes it all clear. The story goes that our Saviour went into a baker's shop, where they were baking, and asked for some bread to eat. The mistress of the shop immediately put a piece of dough into the oven to bake for Him, but was reprimanded by her daughter, who, insisting that the piece of dough was too large, reduced it to a very small size. The dough, however, immediately afterwards began to swell, and presently became a most enormous loaf; whereupon the baker's daughter cried out : 'Heugh! heugh! heugh!' which owl-like noise probably induced our Saviour to transform her into that bird. This tradition is also current in Wales; but, there, the baker's daughter altogether refuses to give Jesus a bit of dough, for which He changed her into the *Cassek gwenwyn, lilith, lamia, strix,* the night-spectre, *mara,* the screech-owl.

In the catalogue of the pictures at Kenilworth,

170

Legends about Bread

belonging to Queen Elizabeth's Earl of Leicester at the time of his death (September 4, 1588), are 'The Picture of King Philip, with a Curtaine,' and 'The Picture of the Baker's Daughter, with a Curtaine.' And he had a copy of the same, or another picture of 'The Baker's Daughter,' at his house at Wanstead. Whether this was a picture of the foregoing legend or not, no one can tell; but it has been suggested, from the fact of King Philip and the baker's daughter coming in sequence in the catalogue, that it was the portrait of a female respecting whom there was some scandal current during Mary's lifetime; it being said in an old ballad that Philip loved

> ' The baker's daughter, in her russet gown,
>   Better than Queen Mary, with her crown.'

Here is another story of miraculous bread. The *Mirakel Steeg* (Miracle Street), at Leyden, derives its name from a miracle which happened there in 1315, and which is thus related in the *Kronyk van Holland van den Klerk :* 'In the aforesaid year of famine, in the town of Leyden, there occurred a signal miracle to two women who lived next door to each other ; for one having bought a barley loaf she cut it into two pieces and laid one half by, for that was all her living, because of the great dearness and famine that prevailed. And as she stood, and was cutting off the one half for her children, her neighbour, who was in great want and need through hunger, saw her, and begged her, for God's sake, to give her the other half, and she would pay her well. But she denied again and again, and affirmed mightily and by oath that

she had no other bread, and as her neighbour would
not believe her, she said in an angry mood: "If I
have any bread in my house more than this, I pray
God that it may turn to stone." Then her neighbour
left her and went away. But when the first half of
the loaf was eaten up, and she went for the other half
which she had laid by, that bread was become stone,
which stone, just as the bread was, is now at Leyden,
at St. Peter's Church, and as a sign they are wont, on
all high feast days, to lay it before the Holy Ghost.'

A stone loaf, supposed to be this one, is now shown
at the hospital in Middelburg, where, in the vestibule,
hangs an old picture representing the miracle at
Leyden. The original stone loaf, it is believed,
disappeared from Leyden about the time of the
Reformation.

Of all extraordinary uses to which a loaf of bread
could be put is that of 'sin eating,' by which, at a
funeral, a man was found who would for a small fee
eat a loaf of bread, in the eating of which he was
supposed to take the dead man's sins upon himself.
In a letter from John Bagford, a famous bookseller,
dated February 1, 1714–15, relating to the antiquities
of London, which is printed in Leland's *Collectanea*,
he says: 'Within the memory of our fathers in
Shropshire, in those villages adjoyning to Wales,
when a person dyed there was notice given to an old
sire (for so they called him), who presently repaired
to the place where the deceased lay, and stood before
the door of the house, when some of the family came
out and furnished him with a cricket, on which he
sat down, facing the door. Then they gave him a

Legends about Bread

groat, which he put in his pocket ; a crust of bread, which he eat ; and a full bowle of ale, which he drank off at a draught. After this he got up from the cricket and pronounced, with a composed gesture, *the ease and rest of the soul departed, for which he would pawn his own soul.* This I had from the ingenious John Aubrey, Esq., who made a collection of curious observations, which I have seen, and is now remaining in the hands of Mr. Churchill, the bookseller. How can a man think otherwise of this than it proceeded from the ancient heathens ? '

This MS. of Aubrey's, of which Bagford speaks, is, most probably, that now preserved in the British Museum (Lansdowne MSS. 231) entitled ' Romains of Gentilisme and Judaisme,' and dated February, 1686–7. In it he thus writes :

' SINNE-EATERS.—In the County of Hereford was an old custom at funeralls to have poor people, who were to take upon them all the sinnes of the party deceased. One of them, I remember, lived in a cottage on Rosse Highway. (He was a long, lean, ugly, lamentable poor raskal.) The manner was, that when the Corps was brought out of the house, and layd on the Biere, a Loafe of bread was brought out, and delivered to the Sinne-eater over the corps, as also a Mazar-bowle of Maple (Gossips' bowle) full of beer, which he was to drinke up, and sixpence in money, in consideration whereof he tooke upon him (*ipso facto*) all the Sinnes of the Defunct, and freed him (or her) from walking after they were dead. This custome alludes (methinkes) something to the Scapegoate in ye old Lawe. Leviticus, cap. xvi.

verse 21-22: "And Aaron shall lay both his hands on the head of the live goate, and confesse over him all ye iniquities of the children of Israel, and all their transgressions in all their sins, putting them upon the head of the goat, and shall send him away, by the hand of a fitt man, into the wildernesse." This custome (though rarely used in our dayes) yet by some people was continued even in the strictest time of ye Presbyterian government; as at Dynder, *nolens volens* the Parson of ye Parish, the relations of a woman deceased there had the ceremonie punctually performed according to her Will; also the like was done at ye City of Hereford, in these times, when a woman kept, manie yeares before her death, a Mazard bowle for the sinne-eater; and the like as in other places in this Countie, as also in Brecon, *e.g.*, at Llangors, where Mr. Givin, the minister, about 1640, could no hinder ye performing of this ancient custome. I believe this custome was, heretofore, used all over Wales'.

'See *Juvenal*, Satyr vi. (519-521) where he speaks of throwing purple thread into the river to carry away one's sinnes.

'In North Wales the Sinne-eaters are frequently made use of; but there, instead of a Bowle of Beere, they have a bowle of Milke.

'Methinkes, Doles to Poore people with money at Funeralls have some resemblance to that of ye Sinne-eater. Doles at Funeralls were continued at gentlemen's funerals in the West of England till the Civil-warre. And so in Germany at rich men's funerals Doles are in use, and to everyone a quart of strong and good beer.'

Legends about Bread

Anent these doles, Pennant says it was customary, when the corpse was brought out of the house and laid upon the bier, for the next-of-kin, be it widow, mother, sister, or daughter (for it must be a female), to give over the coffin a quantity of white loaves in a great dish, and sometimes a cheese, with a piece of money stuck in it, to certain poor persons. After that they presented in the same manner a cup of drink, and required the person to drink a little of it immediately.

Sin-eating survived the times of Aubrey and Bagford, for in a book, *Christmas Evans, the Preacher of Wild Wales*, by the Rev. Paxton Hood, Lond., 1881, he says : 'The superstition of the Sin-eater is said to linger, even now, in the secluded vale of Cwm-Aman, in Carmarthenshire. The meaning of this most singular institution of superstition was, that when a person died, the friends sent for the Sin-Eater of the district, who, on his arrival, placed a plate of salt and bread on the breast of the deceased person ; he then uttered an incantation over the bread, after which he proceeded to eat it, thereby eating the sins of the dead person ; this done, he received a fee of two and sixpence, which, we suppose, was much more than many a preacher received for a long and painful service. Having received this, he vanished as quickly as possible, all the friends and relatives of the departed aiding his exit with blows and kicks, and other indications of their faith in the service he had rendered. A hundred years since, and through the ages before that time, we suppose this curious superstition was everywhere prevalent.'

175

The History of Bread

Bread and salt are used in several ways. In Russia, Servia, and wherever the Greek Church holds sway, they are presented to honoured guests as a welcome. The custom even obtains in England. A correspondent of *Notes and Queries* (5 Series ix. 48), says : 'Some years since I called for the first time on Canon Percy, of Carlisle, at his residence there. When refreshments had been offered and declined, he said : "You must have some bread and salt," with some remarks to imply that it was the way to establish a friendship. These were then brought in and eaten, without anything to lead one to suppose that this was an unusual custom in the house.'

There was another curious custom in the North of England, as another correspondent shows in the same volume (p. 138) : 'In the North Riding, 20 or 30 years ago, a roll of new bread, a pinch of table salt, and a new silver groat, or fourpenny-piece, were offered to every babe on its first visit to a friend's house. The gift was certainly made, more than once, to me, and I recollect seeing it made to other babies. The groat was reserved for its proper owner, but the nurse, who carried that owner, appropriated the bread and salt, and was gratified with a half-crown or so.' Several other correspondents confirm this, and somewhat enlarge upon it, including in the gift an egg and a match. One (5 Ser. x. 216) thus explains the custom : 'The custom of presenting an egg, etc., is widely distributed. I can answer for it in Lincolnshire, Yorkshire, and Durham. In Lincolnshire, at the first visit of a new baby at a friendly house, it is presented with " an egg, both meat and drink ; salt,

Legends about Bread

which savours everything; bread, the staff of life; a match, to light it through the world; and a coin, that it may never want money." This is the case at Winterton, where it is still done. In Durham, a piece of christening-cake is hidden under the child's robe, and given to the first person of the opposite sex met on coming out of church. This is wholly distinct from the egg presentation.' It is common at Edinburgh, and in other parts of Scotland, to give bread and cheese, on the Sabbath, to the first person of the opposite sex met with when the baby is taken to church to be baptised.

One of the most peculiar uses to which a loaf of bread could be put is the discovery of the bodies of drowned persons. The earliest instance I can find is in the *Gentleman's Magazine* for 1767, p. 189. (It is also in the *Annual Register* for the same year.) 'Wednesday, April 8.—An inquisition was taken, at Newbery, Berks, on the body of a child, near two years old, who fell into the river Kennet and was drowned. The jury brought in their verdict, Accidental death. The body was discovered by a very singular experiment, which was as follows: After diligent search had been made in the river for the child, to no purpose, a twopenny leaf, with a quantity of quicksilver put into it, was set floating from the place where the child, it was supposed, had fallen in, which steered its course down the river, upwards of half a mile, before a great number of spectators, when the body, happening to lay on the contrary side of the river, the loaf suddenly tacked about, and swam across the river, and gradually sunk near the child, when both the child and loaf were immediately brought up with grubbers ready for that purpose.'

This superstition has survived till modern times, as the following three or four instances will show. On January 24, 1872, a boy named Harris fell into the stream at Sherborne, Dorsetshire, near Dark Hole Mill, and was drowned. The body not having been found for some days, the following expedient was adopted to discover its whereabouts : On January 30, a four-pound loaf, of the best flour, was procured, and a small piece cut out of its side, forming a cavity, into which a little quicksilver was poured. The piece was then replaced and tied firmly in its original position. The loaf, thus prepared, was then thrown into the river at the spot where the boy fell in, and was expected to float down the stream until it came to the place where the body was supposed to have lodged, when it began to eddy round and round, thus indicating the sought-for spot ; but on this occasion there was no result.

A writer in *Notes and Queries*, January 3, 1878, p. 8, says : 'A young woman has singularly disappeared at Swinton, near Sheffield. The canal has been unsuccessfully dragged, and the Swinton folk are now going to test the merits of a local superstition which afirms that a loaf of bread containing quicksilver, if cast upon the water, will drift to, keep afloat, and remain stationary over any dead body which may be lying immersed out of sight.'

The *Leeds Mercury*, October 26, 1883, has the following : 'A Press Association despatch says : Adelaide Amy Terry, servant to Dr. Williams, of

Legends about Bread

Brentford, was sent to a neighbour with a message on Sunday evening, and as she did not return, and was known to be short-sighted, it was feared she had fallen into the canal, which was dragged, but without success. On Tuesday an old bargewoman suggested that a loaf of bread, in which some quicksilver had been placed, should be floated in the water. This was done, and the loaf became stationary at a certain spot. The dragging was resumed there, and the body was discovered.'

The following is from the *Stamford Mercury*, December 18, 1885: 'At Ketton, on Tuesday, an inquest was held by Mr. Shield, coroner, touching the death of Harry Baker, aged twenty-three, who was missed on the night of November 27, after the termination of the polling for the county election, and was believed to have walked into the ford, near the stone bridge, during the darkness. The river at that time was running strongly, and deceased had no companions with him. The dragging-irons from Stamford were obtained, and a protracted search was made in the river, but without result. However, in obedience to the wish of Baker's mother, a loaf charged with quicksilver (said to have been scraped from an old looking-glass) was cast upon the waters, and it came to a standstill in the river at the bottom of Mr. Lewin's field. Here the grappling-hooks were put in, and at four o'clock on Monday afternoon last the corpse was brought to the surface, having been in the water seventeen days. The river had been dragged several times before at this spot.'

Nor is this superstition confined to England, for

The History of Bread

in Brittany, when the body of a drowned man cannot be found, a lighted taper is fixed in a loaf consecrated to St. Nicholas, which is then abandoned to the retreating current, and where the loaf stops there they expect to find the body. In Germany the name of the drowned person is inscribed on the bread. And a somewhat similar idea seems to obtain among the Canadian Indians, for Sir Jas. E. Alexander, in his *L'Acadie* (p. 26), says: 'The Indians imagine that in the case of a drowned body its place may be discovered by floating a chip of cedar-wood, which will stop and turn round over the exact spot. An instance occurred within my own knowledge in the case of Mr. Lavery, of Kingston Mill, whose boat overset, and the person was drowned near Cedar Island ; nor could the body be discovered until the experiment was resorted to.'

Aubrey (*Remains of Gentilisme and Judaisme*) says he had the following from old Mr. Frederick Vaughan : 'The Friar's Mendicant heretofore would take their opportunity to come to the houses when the good woemen did bake, and would *read a Ghospel over the batch*, and the good woman would give them a cake, etc. It should seem by Chaucer's tale that they had a fashion to beg in rhyme—

> " Of your white bread I would desire a shiver,
> And of your hen, the liver." '

And Aubrey's friend, Dr. White Kennet, says in the same book : ' In Kent and many other parts the women when they have kneaded their dough into a loaf cut ye form of a cross on the top of it.'

Legends about Bread

I have been favoured by the Rev. T. F. Thiselton-Dyer, whose works on folk-lore are so deservedly well known, with the following notes on superstitions about bread :

'Throughout the world a special respect has always been paid to bread as the "staff of life." Hence, according to a trite and common saying: "The man who wastes bread will live to want." It is not surprising, indeed, that this food of man, which in some form or other is indispensable, should have from time immemorial been invested with an almost sacred character, anyone who is recklessly careless of the household loaf incurring risk of poverty one day himself.

'At the outset, it may be noticed that, as a precautionary measure against mishaps of any kind, many housewives were formerly in the habit of making the sign of the cross on their loaves of bread before placing them in the ovens, a practice which is still kept up in some parts of the country. Various explanations have been assigned for this custom, the common one being "that it prevents the bread turning out heavy." In Shropshire one day remarked an elderly maidservant: "We always make a cross on the flour before baking, and on the malt before mashing up for brewing. It's to keep it from being bewitched." 'Some, again, maintain that the sign of the cross "keeps the bread from getting mouldy," but, whatever the true reason, it is persistently adhered to in the West of England. As, however, evil spirits and malicious fairies were generally supposed to be powerless when confronted with the sign of the cross, there is every reason to suppose that this is the origin of this superstition.

'In days gone by, too, bread was used as a charm against witches, no doubt from its being stamped with the sign of the holy cross. Herrick, for instance, in his *Hesperides*, alludes to this usage in the following rhyme :

> "Bring the holy crust of bread,
> Lay it underneath the head ;
> 'Tis a certain charm to keep
> Hags away while children sleep."

'Bread, too, has long been employed as a physical charm for the cure of various complaints. Thus, an old book, entitled *A Work for Householders*, written in the early part of the 16th century, gives this charm as in use for the toothache. "The Charmer taketh a piece of white bread, and saith over that bread the Pater Noster, and maketh a cross upon the bread ; then doth he lay that piece of bread upon the tooth that acheth or unto any sore, turning the cross unto the sore or disease, and so is the person healed." Then there was the famous Good Friday bread, which was in request for its medicinal virtues, being considered a sovereign remedy for diarrhœa when grated in a small quantity of water. An anecdote is told of a cottager who lamented that her poor neighbour must certainly die, because she had already given her two doses of this bread, but, unfortunately, without any success. Indeed, in days gone by, so much importance was attached to bread thus baked, that there were in most parts few country houses in which it was not to be found. At the present day also one

may occasionally find the custom kept up, especially
in the Northern counties, where so many of the old
beliefs survive.

'But these are not the only ways in which bread
has been the source of superstition, it having held a
prominent place in numerous curious ceremonies.
Thus sailors used it as offerings to propitiate the
elements; and we are told how the seafaring
community of Greece, in the 17th century, were accustomed to take to sea 30 loaves of bread, consecrated
and named St. Nicholas' loaves. In case of a storm
these were thrown into the sea one by one, until they
had succeeded in calming the waves.

'Oblations of this kind were of frequent occurrence
in past years. The Russian sailor, in order to appease
the angry spirit that troubled the waters of the White
Sea, would cast into the water a small cake or loaf
made of flour and butter. Again, a Norwegian story
states that a sailor wished, according to custom, to
give on Christmas Day a cake to the spirit that
presided over the waters; but, when he came to the
shore, lo! the waters were frozen over. Unwilling to
leave his little offering on the ice, the sailor tried to
make a hole; but in spite of all his efforts it was
not large enough for him to put his cake through.
Suddenly, to his surprise, a tiny hand, as white as
snow, was stretched through the hole, and seizing the
offering withdrew with it.

'To give a further illustration, we are told by a
correspondent of *Mélusine* (Jan., 1885) that in the
Isle de Sein "a little ship made of bread crusts is
suspended over the table, and on Holy Thursday it

The History of Bread

is lowered down and burnt, while all uncover and the *Veni Creator* is sung. Another bread ship is then suspended over the table. This ceremony is known as the Ship Feast, and is designed to insure the safety of the family fishing boat." Among further beliefs current among sailors in our own country is the notion that it is unlucky to turn a loaf upside down after helping oneself from it, the idea being that for every loaf so turned a ship will be wrecked. It is also said that if a loaf parts in the hand while being cut it bodes dissensions in the family—the separation of husband and wife.

'Once more, bread is not without its many traditions and legendary lore. According to a popular tale told of the City of Stavoreen, Holland, there resided in it a certain rich virgin, who owned many ships. One day she entertained a wizard, but gave him no bread. In consequence of this serious omission he predicted her downfall, remarking that bread was the most useful and necessary thing. Soon after a shipmaster was bidden to procure the most valuable cargo in the world. He chose a load of wheat ; but, on arriving with his cargo, he was ordered to throw it overboard. It was in vain that he begged to be allowed to give it to the poor. Accordingly it was thrown into the sea; but the wheat sprouted, and a bank grew up, the harbour being ruined for ever. A Welsh legend tells how, many years ago, a man who dwelt in the parish of Myddvai saw three beautiful nymphs in the water, and courted them. They, however, called him "Eater of Hard-baked Bread," and refused to have anything

Legends about Bread

to do with him. One day, however, he saw floating on the lake a substance resembling unbaked bread, which he fished up and ate, and was thereby possessed of one of the lovely water-nymphs.

'Thus, in one form or another, bread can boast of an extensive and widespread folk-lore, besides having in our own and other countries been made the subject of numerous proverbs, many of which are well-known from daily use as incorporating familiar truths. The common saying, for instance, which says : Never turn a loaf in the presence of a Menteith,' originated with Sir Walter Scott, in his *Tales by a Grandfather*, thus : Sir John Stewart de Menteith was the person who betrayed Sir William Wallace to King Edward. His signal was, when he turned a loaf set upon the table, the guests were to rush on the patriot and seize him. Then there is the phrase, "to cut large slices out of another man's loaf," referring to those who look after themselves at their neighbour's expense. A popular Scotch proverb tells us that "Bread's house skailed never"; in other words, a full or hospitable house never wants visitors ; and, according to another old proverb, "Bread and milk is bairns' meat, I wish them sorry that lo'e it." '

THE END.

LONDON :
PRINTED BY WILLIAM CLOWES AND SONS, LIMITED,
DUKE STREET, STAMFORD STREET, S.E., AND GREAT WINDMILL STREET, W.

opular Natural History of the Lower Animals.
Invertebrates.
By HENRY SCHERREN, F.Z.S.,
Author of 'Through a Pocket Lens,' etc.

With 169 Illustrations. Crown 8vo. Cloth. 3s 6d.

It gives in simple language many details concerning the structure and habits 'backboneless animals." The text is profusely illustrated, and altogether the plication is a practical elementary treatise on the invertebrates.'—*The Morning*
st

It is carefully written, and quite intelligible to the ignorant. An excellent dbook.'—*The British Weekly*.

Interspersed with a large number of scientific facts will be found a quantity of using reading.'—*The Field*.

Creatures of the Sea.
Being the Life Stories of Some Sea Birds, Beasts, and Fishes.
By FRANK T. BULLEN, F.R.G.S.,
Author of 'The Cruise of the "Cachalot,"' etc.

With Forty Illustrations by THEO. CARRERAS.

Demy 8vo. Cloth gilt, gilt top, 7s. 6d.

r Bullen takes his readers long and pleasant voyages over the vast expanse of Ocean, and enables them to see with something of his own keenness of observa- and sympathetic interest the wonderful varieties of animate life that are found n and beneath its mighty waters. *Those familiar with Mr. Bullen's style ily need to be told that there is nothing of the dry scientific character about these 'ies His vivid and glowing pictures of the wonderful and varied life of the b Sea possess a human and lifelike quality often absent from the elaborate riptions of severer scientific and technical treatises.*

The Trees and Plants of the Bible.
By W. H. GROSER, B.Sc.

Illustrated. Cloth. 2s.

part from its religious value, this little volume must approve itself to all rs of botany.'—*The Times*.

The Animals of the Bible.
By H. CHICHESTER HART,
Naturalist to Sir G. Nares' Arctic Expedition and Professor Hull's
Palestine Expedition.

Illustrated. Cloth. 2s.

ne feels in reading the book that much of the information has been obtained st hand.'—*The Schoolmaster*.
capital handbook for teachers.'—*The Saturday Review*..

Plants of the Bible.
By Rev. GEORGE HENSLOW, M.A., F.L.S., etc.
Illustrated from Photographs of the Plants themselves.

Foolscap 8vo. Cloth. 1s.

brief but reasonable introduction to Scriptural botany.'—*The Manchester dian*.

SOME STANDARD WORKS.

The Bible Handbook.

An Introduction to the Study of Holy Scripture.

By the late JOSEPH ANGUS, D.D.

New Edition thoroughly Revised, and in part Re-written by
SAMUEL G. GREEN, D.D.

Author of 'A Handbook of Church History,' etc.

Large crown 8vo. Cloth gilt. 6s. net.

The Tabernacle.

Its History and Structure.

By the Rev. W. SHAW CALDECOTT.

With a preface by Professor SAYCE, LL.D.

With a Map and Eighteen Illustrations and Diagrams.

Large crown 8vo. Cloth gilt. 5s.

In regard to the precise form of the Tabernacle, so much necessarily depended upon a true understanding of the various linear measures of the Old Testament, that reconstruction was always attended with some doubt. Mr. Caldecott believes, however, that he has solved the last difficulty. The Bible reader will find the volume of absorbing interest. Its text is freely illustrated by maps and plans specially prepared for the work. Professor Sayce contributes a commendatory Preface.

A Handbook of Church History.

From the Apostolic Era to the Dawn of the Reformation.

By SAMUEL G. GREEN, D.D.

Author of 'A Handbook of Old Testament Hebrew,' etc.

With Full Dates, Chronological Tables, and Index.

640 pages. 6s. net.

For the purposes of the student it will be found simple in arrangement, lucid in style, and entirely without bias; while careful chronological and other tables will facilitate its use as a text-book. At the same time the history is eminently adapted for the general reader, who will find a subject, which is often rendered for him unapproachable by the dry and technical method of its treatment, dealt with in a style at once popular and exact.

'It is a capable and lucid narrative, which seems to succeed in treating a history which covers 14½ centuries in not too sketchy a manner, and which is not intent in establishing any partizan doctrine.'—*The Times.*

'It is an interesting synoptic view of the history of the Western Church.'—*The Daily News.*

'It gives an able and interesting presentation of a subject which has often been made repellant by the manner in which it was treated.'—*The Scotsman.*

'It is a marvel of cheapness.'—*The Glasgow Herald.*

LONDON: THE RELIGIOUS TRACT SOCIETY.

The Slave in History.

His Sorrows and his Emancipation.

By WILLIAM STEVENS,

Some time Editor of *The Leisure Hour.*

With Portraits and with Six Illustrations by J. FINNEMORE, R.A.

Large Crown 8vo. Cloth gilt. 6s.

In this work Mr. Stevens presents a vivid picture of the life and circumstances of ie slave in all ages and lands. The influence of Christianity on the slave life, and ie steps by which Christian nations successfully shook themselves free from ɔmplicity in slave-holding are carefully detailed; whilst the chief workers in the reat emancipation movements of modern times are in turn brought before the ·ader's attention. *The volume furnishes at once the most comprehensive and the* ıost up-to-date survey of the slavery question. The illustrations include some ivid pictures of slave-life, and incidents in the emancipation movement.

The China Martyrs of 1900.

ⁱ Complete Roll of the Christian Heroes Martyred in China in 1900, with Narratives of Survivors.

Compiled and Edited by ROBERT COVENTRY FORSYTH,

For 18 years a Missionary in China of the Baptist Missionary Society.

With 144 Portraits and other Illustrations.

Demy 8vo. Cloth gilt. 7s. 6d.

This volume seeks to place on record in a permanent form a complete account f the terrible convulsion in China in the year 1900, known as the Boxer Move-ient. It contains the thrilling story of how death, for Christ's sake, was bravely iet in many of its most hideous forms by missionaries and native Christians like. *It also describes some of the most miraculous escapes from death on the* ɔrt of missionaries and native Christians. The story of the siege of Peking is escribed from a Christian point of view, and the author sums up his study of the reat episode in the conviction that in China of to-day, as in other parts of the orld in all ages, the blood of the martyrs will prove to be the seed of the Church.

Thirty Years in Madagascar.

By the Rev. T. T. MATTHEWS,

Of the London Missionary Society.

With Sixty-Two Portraits and other Illustrations from Photographs and Sketches. Demy 8vo. Cloth gilt. 6s.

'Mr. Matthews' story forms a splendid record of good work accomplished, and ie volume is by far the most interesting and entertaining of all the books which ave been published lately concerning missionary life in the great African island.'
The Athenæum.
'It is a remarkab e record of Christian activity '—*The Pall Mall Gazette.*
'The n⁺ ins worth of the book ought to ensure its success, for it takes a place ⁱɪt⁻ ʊⱱ n among M.-sionary volumes '—*The Examiner.*

LONDON: THE RELIGIOUS TRACT SOCIETY.

BIOGRAPHICAL WORKS.

Champions of the Truth.

Short Lives of Christian Leaders in Thought and Action. By various Writers.

Edited by A. R. BUCKLAND, M.A.

With Portraits. Crown 8vo. Cloth gilt. 3s. 6d.

'Here are pen portraits of eighteen Evangelical teachers, beginning with Wyclif and ending with Spurgeon. It need hardly be said, perhaps, that their eighteen biographers treat them from about the same point of view. The admirable thing is that, though that point of view is one with which a given reader may not be so fortunate as to find himself in sympathy, it is one which has the advantage of showing the subject of the biography at his best. A very pleasant volume, and the more to be valued for the sake of its fifteen portraits.'—*The Academy.*

Hugh Latimer.

By ROBERT DEMAUS, M.A.

Author of 'William Tindale,' etc.

New Edition, Revised. With a Portrait. Large crown 8vo. Cloth gilt. 3s. 6d.

The First Edition of this work was published by the Society in 1869, but so careful was the Author in his method and research that it still ranks as the STANDARD LIFE OF THE GREAT REFORMER.

The Homes and Haunts of Luther.

By JOHN STOUGHTON, D.D.

Third Edition. Thoroughly Revised by C. H. IRWIN, M.A.

With Eleven Illustrations. Crown 8vo. Cloth gilt. 2s. 6d.

Several new Illustrations appear in this Third Edition, including a fine reproduction of a very rare portrait of Luther by Cranach. The reviser's notes contain a considerable amount of new material, especially in regard to Wittenberg and the restoration of its historic Castle Church.

'The teaching of this sturdy Protestant Reformer re-shaped the Religious history of the world; and the story of his life as told in these fascinating pages cannot be too often enforced.'—*The Record.*

LONDON: THE RELIGIOUS TRACT SOCIETY.

CPSIA information can be obtained
at www.ICGtesting.com
Printed in the USA
LVOW13*0713291017

554137LV00015BA/291/P

9 781298 758132